28 Days Keto

A complete guide to living the
keto lifestyle easily

Lisa Butterworth & Caroline Hwang
Photography by Julia Stotz

28 Days Keto

A complete guide to living the
keto lifestyle easily

Smith
Street
Books

CONTENTS

INTRODUCTION

You have probably heard a lot about keto, or the ketogenic diet – from your neighbour who lost 14 kg (31 lb) in as many days, your co-worker who snacks on macadamias from morning to night, or your friend who declines dessert at every gathering. But what is keto, and why would someone want to eat this way?

Although the phrase 'ketogenic diet' was coined in the 1920s by an American physician and researcher, this particular way of eating – high in fat, low in carbohydrates and with moderate protein – gained mainstream popularity as a weight-loss measure in the 1970s, and in the last several years has become a top wellness trend.

What keto is not is a quick 'fix'. For many people who eat keto, it is less a diet than a lifestyle. To shift the way your body produces energy, from using glucose to converting ketones, takes a regimented way of eating and a commitment to doing so. But once you do, the health benefits – including weight loss – can be plentiful.

The first step towards eating a ketogenic diet is to have an understanding of the state of ketosis, and how your body gets there. Once you are familiar with the process, it is time to figure out the proper percentages and amounts of your dietary elements (there is a general formula that can be individually adapted). After you have a good grasp of this, you will likely want to empty your pantry of its current non-keto staples, and replenish it with items that support this high-fat, low-carb, medium-protein way of eating. Once you have taken all of these steps, you are primed to begin prepping meals and eating ketogenically. Clearly there is nothing quick about it. The amount of information to digest, calculations to make and daily meals and snacks to prepare can feel quite overwhelming (not to mention some of the unpleasant symptoms that might arise during your transition), which is why this book is broken down into the basics, providing the information you need to eat keto healthily, along with weekly shopping lists, prep tips and daily recipes for doing so. Going keto isn't easy, but this book will make your dietary journey as simple, smooth and delicious as possible.

HOW TO USE THIS BOOK

There are many ways you can incorporate a keto diet into your life: adopt it strictly for an extended period of time, use it short-term to break a pattern of carb- and sugar-dependency or take the parts that work best for you and apply them to a generally low-carb lifestyle, whether you aim to keep the body in ketosis or not. This book provides the tools you need to explore and experiment with this way of eating, including the understanding of what going keto means, and why it has the effects and benefits that it does.

Most importantly, this book provides a blueprint for 28 days' worth of wonderfully satiating and delightfully flavourful keto-friendly meals, organised to include a recipe for breakfast, lunch and dinner with a daily macronutrient breakdown that adheres to keto parameters. In order to make your introduction into keto as easy as possible, the days are organised by weeks, and each week includes a shopping list as well as helpful prep tips, because planning and prepping are two of the major keys to going keto successfully without feeling discouraged and restricted.

In addition to recipes for daily meals are a number of basic recipes, such as cauliflower rice and zucchini (courgette) noodles ('zoodles'), that will help set you up for daily success, along with keto-friendly sauces, dressings and condiments. And because having high-fat snacks on hand is crucial in sticking to a keto diet, there are a number of delicious, nutrient-dense snack recipes as well. You can use this 28-day meal plan to kick off your keto life, come back to it whenever you want a strictly keto refresh, and pick and choose your favourite recipes to make again and again as you continue your keto journey.

Keep in mind that these recipes are based on the macronutrient needs of the average person (more on that later). You may find that you need to adjust your portions, add snacks, tweak the macronutrient ratio depending on your goals and generally adapt the meal plan to best suit your individual needs. Everyone's keto journey is different, but you'll now have the tools to embark on it, and those remain the same whatever your circumstance.

EATING CLEAN

Although eating low-quality items won't keep your body from going into ketosis, which you will soon have a clear understanding of, using high-quality, organic ingredients will ensure you are eating as healthily and cleanly as possible. Whenever possible, choose fresh, organic fruits and vegetables; organic dairy products; grass-fed, pasture-raised meats; and eggs from organic, pasture-raised hens.

WHAT IS KETO?

Of all the wellness trends and eating styles, the ketogenic diet is probably one of the most misunderstood. For starters, it is a diet in which most of the day's calories come from fat, and how can a diet so high in fat (something we have been conditioned to avoid in large quantities) cause weight loss, let alone have health benefits?

To understand the ketogenic diet, and its purpose (to put the body in a metabolic state of ketosis), it's important to first understand the biochemical process of turning food into energy.

CONVERTING FOOD TO ENERGY

In order to stay alive, our body needs energy. Energy is what keeps our cells working, our organs functioning, our systems healthy. This energy comes from the food we eat, which is made up of three macronutrients:

Carbohydrates: Carbohydrates include sugars, starches and fibres found in a number of foods from fruits and vegetables to bread, sweets and dairy products. They fall into two categories: simple carbs (which are absorbed at a quicker rate) like those found in fruit and dairy; and complex carbs (which are digested at a slower rate), such as those found in legumes, grains and starchy vegetables.

Protein: Proteins are essential to our existence, as these compounds made of chains of amino acids (simple organic compounds) support a number of crucial roles in the body, including the proper function of cells and the health of muscles and organs. Proteins are found in meat, dairy products, nuts and legumes.

Fat: Fats are also crucial to our existence and are stored by the body as an energy reserve. Fats protect our organs, provide insulation and help us absorb fat-soluble vitamins including A, D, E and K, which are vital for our overall health. Fats are found in nuts, meat, fish, vegetable oils and dairy products.

Each of these macronutrients can be converted into energy by the body, but carbs are the macronutrient our body turns to first. Every carb we ingest gets broken down into glucose, which enters the circulatory system through the small intestine. Once glucose hits the bloodstream, the pancreas secretes insulin, which tells cells to let the glucose in through the glucose channel, where it is converted to energy. Insulin converts excess glucose into glycogen, some of which is stored in the liver and muscles; any remaining glucose is turned into fat.

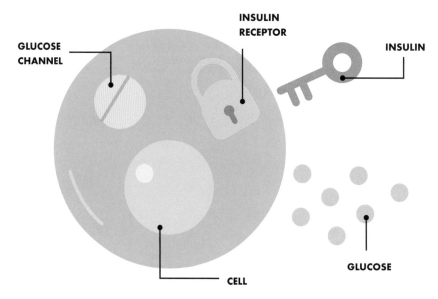

GLUCOSE CHANNEL

INSULIN RECEPTOR

INSULIN

CELL

GLUCOSE

MACRONUTRIENT BREAKDOWNS

To understand how the keto diet differs from the standard Western diet, and why it has the effect on the body that it does, it is necessary to compare the macronutrient breakdown of each group.

STANDARD WESTERN DIET

In a standard Western diet, the breakdown of macronutrient percentages looks like this:

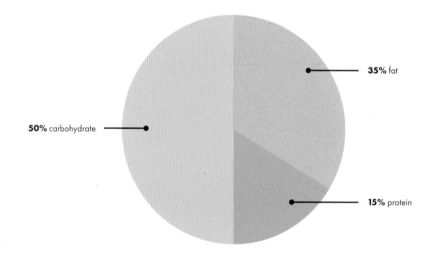

35% fat

50% carbohydrate

15% protein

KETO DIET

In a ketogenic diet, the breakdown of macronutrient percentages is quite different:

It is precisely this difference in macronutrient breakdown that shifts the body into a state of ketosis.

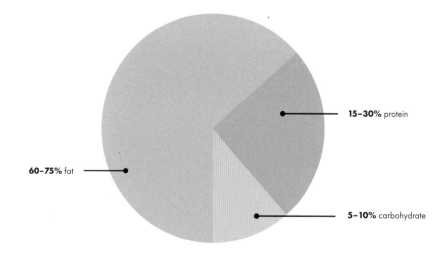

15–30% protein

60–75% fat

5–10% carbohydrate

SAFETY PRECAUTIONS

....

While maintaining a keto diet is considered safe for most people who do it properly and healthfully, eating keto isn't for everyone. In fact, there are certain groups of people who should avoid the keto diet simply because of the changes it creates in your body and its functions. If you have any sort of health condition or are taking prescription medication, be sure to consult your medical practitioner before starting a keto diet.

WOMEN WHO ARE TRYING TO CONCEIVE

If you are preparing your body to be a healthy host for a pregnancy, it is probably not the right time to put your system through such a major change by trying the keto diet.

WOMEN WHO ARE PREGNANT OR BREASTFEEDING

As for women who are pregnant, there is little to no research on the effect of a high-ketone count on a human fetus, so to be on the safe side, it is best to avoid eating a strictly keto diet. The same goes for women who are nursing. There is not much research on the safety of the keto diet while you are breastfeeding, so it is best to eat an adequate amount of carbohydrates, rather than reducing your carb intake drastically while you are nursing.

CHILDREN

A keto diet is very restrictive, something children under the age of 18 should probably not be subjected to. Many are picky enough as it is when it comes to eating, and because of their rapid growth and development, they should have the full range of calories and nutrients available to them through whole grains, proteins, fruits and vegetables.

THE ELDERLY

The elderly should also be wary when considering eating keto, as the rapid weight loss it can cause can be more detrimental than beneficial.

PEOPLE WITH A HISTORY OF DISORDERED EATING

Because of the strict parameters of a keto diet, it is probably not the best option for those who have a history of disordered eating.

ANYONE WITH IMPAIRED KIDNEY OR LIVER FUNCTION OR WITHOUT A GALLBLADDER

Because of the roles the kidneys, liver and gallbladder play in metabolising fat and protein, those who might have problems with these particular organs should consult a medical practitioner before going keto.

DIABETICS

Eating a keto diet can be very beneficial for those with diabetes, particularly type 2 diabetes, which is typically associated with insulin resistance and affects the way the body's system processes glucose in the bloodstream. Those with type 1 diabetes, a chronic disease affecting the pancreas so that it makes little to no insulin, should be especially careful when considering a keto diet, as everyone reacts differently to a low-carb, high-fat diet, and the results could be dangerous if your insulin production is already compromised. Anyone with type 1 or type 2 diabetes should consult a medical practitioner before trying a keto diet, and should do so with continued supervision from a doctor and/or nutritionist.

WESTERN DIET WOES

Before we dive deeper into the effects of eating a ketogenic diet, we need to look at the typical way many people in modern, urbanised Western countries eat, also known as the Western diet (in the US it is referred to as the Standard American Diet, which has a very apt acronym: SAD).

WHAT IS THE WESTERN DIET?

Lots of fried, processed and packaged foods, ample amounts of red meat and refined grains create the bulk of the Western diet, along with a dearth of plant-based fibre, i.e., fruits and vegetables. In other words, it is a diet high in fat (the unhealthy kind, more on that later), sugar and sodium, and low in fibre and all the vitamins and nutrients available in fresh produce. If you take a look at the chart on page 12, you will see that it is also a diet that gets most of its calories from carbohydrates. As if the staples of this diet and the type of energy they create weren't problematic enough, folks who eat the foods of a Western diet tend to eat way more of them than necessary, which creates its own host of issues.

HEALTH ISSUES & THE WESTERN DIET

Our bodies aren't fans of highly processed foods. In fact some of the ingredients, such as fructose, a type of simple sugar, can elicit a response from our immune system, reducing its effectiveness in battling other harmful entities and causing low-grade inflammation, which typically doesn't have any outward symptoms but can lead to lots of issues such as heart disease.

Forcing our bodies to digest lots of processed foods can also lead to a change in our gut flora, reducing the good bacteria, which makes our systems run smoothly and upping the bad, causing digestive and nutrient absorption issues.

A carb-heavy diet also causes spikes in our blood sugar. A carb-heavy meal throws a lot of glucose into the bloodstream. The pancreas responds by pumping out insulin in order to move the glucose in our bloodstream to our cells for use, and all the excess into storage. But that glucose spike, and the subsequent insulin spike, can also remove too much glucose from the bloodstream, causing what we know as a sugar crash. Taxing our systems like this can eventually lead to insulin resistance, a precursor to type 2 diabetes. And what about all that extra glucose? It gets turned into fat.

INSULIN RESISTANCE

After decades of extreme glucose spikes, the body's response to insulin (which also spikes) can become impaired, leading to the body's inability to properly regulate the levels of glucose in the bloodstream. This can lead to type 2 diabetes, and many associated health issues including eye complications, neuropathy and high blood pressure.

KETOSIS & KETO-ADAPTATION

When the body no longer has a steady supply of carbohydrates, it begins converting fat for energy. The idea is simple, but the biochemical process is a bit more complicated. Our body turns the fat we eat into fatty acids, which enter into our circulatory system through the walls of our small intestine, just like carbohydrates.

When our body has no carbs to burn, it turns to this dietary fat as well as the stored fat in our bodies. Many cells in our body can use fatty acids directly, but some – our brain cells, for instance – cannot. In order to make fatty acids available for energy to the cells that cannot use them directly, our body creates ketone bodies, aka ketones. Ketones are present in our blood, even when our body is using carbohydrates for energy. But when the liver no longer has access to the glucose from carbohydrates – when a person is fasting, exercising for a long time or eating a very low-carb diet – it begins metabolising fat. Through a process known as beta-oxidation, the liver breaks down fat into glycerol and fatty acids. To make the fatty acids useable, the body breaks them down in a process called ketogenesis to produce ketones, the energy-rich compound that provides fuel to the brain, muscles and other tissues. The body needs a little glucose, but it doesn't need to get it from carbohydrates. The body turns the glycerol created during beta-oxidisation into glucose (gluconeogenesis). Ketosis describes this metabolic state of raised ketone bodies in your system. Keto-adaptation is the goal, when your body has adjusted to the shift in energy conversion and is using fat and ketones, instead of glucose, as its main fuel source.

1. Low carbohydrates
a keto diet reduces carb intake

2. Blood glucose
levels of glucose & insulin
in the blood drop

3. More ketones
are present in bloodstream

4. The body
begins breaking down fat instead

5. Ketone
levels in the bloodstream rise

6. Brain & rest of body
uses ketones for energy
instead of glucose

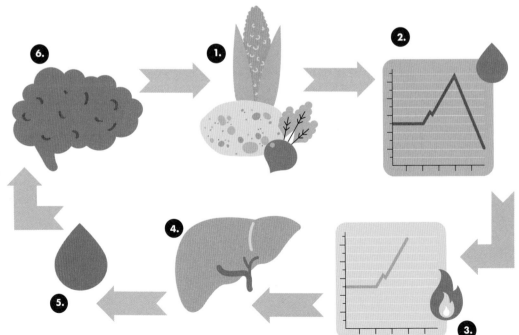

THE DIFFERENCE BETWEEN KETOSIS & KETOACIDOSIS

....

When exploring the ketogenic diet, there's one very important distinction to make: the difference between ketosis and ketoacidosis.

Nutritional ketosis: This refers to the metabolic state of ketones in the system that can be safely entered into and maintained through an intentional, healthy and prolonged high-fat, low-carb, medium-protein diet.

Diabetic ketoacidosis (DKA): This is a life-threatening metabolic state that should be treated immediately. Insulin plays a major role in the regulation of glucose, helping to convert it to energy that cells can use. Ketoacidosis happens most often in people with type 1 diabetes, who do not produce enough insulin to properly regulate glucose; rather than converting glucose to energy, the glucose remains in the blood and the body, still in need of energy, turns to fat for fuel. Using fat for fuel results in the production of ketones, which, if they aren't being properly used for energy, can build up in the blood. This high level of ketones (at least three times higher than that of someone in a state of nutritional ketosis) paired with high blood sugar (as opposed to the low blood sugar state of nutritional ketosis) leads to ketoacidosis. Symptoms can include shortness of breath, vomiting, excessive thirst, fatigue, abdominal pain and frequent urination. Those with type 1 diabetes should consult a doctor before embarking on a ketogenic diet.

KETONES LEVEL CHART

Urine Ketone Levels	0.6 mmol/L	0.6 mmol/L	0.6–3 mmol/L	3–5 mmol/L	5 mmol/L	10 mmol/L
What do my ketone levels mean?	Normal to low	Beginning ketosis	Nutritional ketosis (ideal for purposeful ketosis)	Starvation ketosis	High risk for ketoacidosis (if blood sugar is greater than 250 mg/dL, call a doctor)	DKA (seek medical attention immediately

Blood Ketone Levels	0.6 mmol/L	0.6 mmol/L	0.6–1.5 mmol/L	1.5–3.0 mmol/L	3 mmol/L
What do my ketone levels mean?	Normal to low	Beginning ketosis	Moderate level	High level, may be at risk for DKA	DKA (seek medical attention immediately)

HOW TO KNOW IF YOU ARE IN KETOSIS

Since a heightened level of ketones in your system is a quantifiable measure by which one can tell if they are in ketosis, it is tempting to actually test those levels (see below). But, as mentioned earlier, simply having ketones in the system doesn't mean your body is efficiently using them for fuel. You have chosen to eat a ketogenic diet in order to feel better and benefit your health, so paying attention to your body, and the way you feel, might be a more representative measure of how going keto is working for you.

This is especially true since the levels of ketones, and the body's ability to efficiently process them, can vary between individuals. Some people might experience signs of ketosis after several days to a week of eating a dedicated ketogenic diet. For others it might take longer. But if you are new to the world of keto, and are just embarking on this dietary adventure, testing your level of ketones can help confirm whether you are producing them or not. Because staying in ketosis can be a delicate balance, testing your ketones is another informational tool that can be used to adjust and adapt your diet as your ketogenic journey progresses.

TESTING FOR KETONES

1. By urine: Urine strips are the most affordable, accessible way to test the level of ketones in your body. The more ketones that are in your blood, the more your body will expel through urine. Exposed strips will turn darker when there are more ketones present. Though this might be a helpful metric in the beginning of your dietary shift, the longer you eat ketogenically, the more efficient your body will get at using ketones for fuel, which means fewer will be passed in your urine.

2. By breath: The level of ketones in your breath can also be measured. Though there are several devices on the market for testing this, they are rather expensive and not widely available.

3. By blood: Blood testing for ketones may be the most accurate method, but it is also the most invasive, as the measurement is taken from a drop of blood procured by a finger prick. There are hand-held devices just for this purpose. The process is more expensive than urine strips (though more accurate), but more affordable than the new-to-market breath meters.

See the chart on page 17 for effective levels of ketones in urine and blood.

THE KETO 'FLU'

Eating a keto diet and changing the way your body produces energy, from glucose to fatty acids and ketones, is a major biological shift, and you will likely have some unpleasant symptoms during the transition before you reap the benefits. The good news is that this keto 'flu', as it is known (because the symptoms are flu-like, it is not an actual virus), is totally normal and temporary.

Not everyone gets the keto 'flu', and those who do, experience a range of severity from mild to acute depending on the individual, but the symptoms are generally the same and aren't debilitating. Though it is unclear exactly why this happens, restricting your intake of carbs will generally lead to withdrawals and imbalances in the body, which can cause headaches, nausea, fatigue, cramping, irritability, insomnia and brain fog. You might also experience some gastrointestinal issues including constipation or, though less common, diarrhoea. These symptoms often start within several days to a week of eating keto, and can last anywhere from several days to a week or two.

Thankfully, there are a number of measures you can take to ease these issues.

ADDRESSING SYMPTOMS

Transition into keto: Depending on your current way of eating, cutting sugar and carbs and greatly increasing your fat intake may be a major change for your body. After a lifetime of high-carb eating, suddenly refraining from them can be a shock to the system. Consider easing into eating ketogenically. Not only will this hopefully lessen any keto 'flu' symptoms, but it will also help get you accustomed to this new way of eating, before you get down to the daily nitty-gritty of counting carbs and grams of fat. Start by eliminating sugar from your diet (including all refined sugars, plus honey, maple syrup, agave, etc.). Cut back on fruit as well and introduce more keto-friendly forms of fat and protein into your diet. After a week of no sugar, cut down on your carbs, including bread, grains, pasta, starchy vegetables, etc. Once you have cut most sugar and carbs out of your diet, and got accustomed to a low-carb, high-fat way of eating, switch to all keto-friendly foods and start tracking your intake.

Stay hydrated: When you begin eating ketogenically, you lose a lot of water weight. It is imperative that you drink plenty of water, always, but especially during the first few days and weeks of a shift to ketogenic eating.

Replenish electrolytes: While drinking regular water is great, you will also want to replenish the many electrolytes you will be losing along with the water weight. Look for water that is fortified with electrolytes (but make sure it doesn't have added sweeteners). Another good way to replenish electrolytes is by adding sea salt to your drinking water and food, and adding food items such as spinach to your diet.

Consider supplements: Because it may be difficult to get certain needed electrolytes (such as magnesium and potassium) with keto-friendly foods, consider taking supplements. Find more information about supplements on page 48.

Eat regularly: When you first cut back on your carbs, make sure you are eating regularly – it is more difficult to stay the keto course if you are suddenly famished and haven't prepared something keto-friendly to eat. Carry keto snacks with you so you don't have a carb emergency. Eventually one of the effects of going keto is a decrease in appetite (which many tout as a benefit). Even so, be sure to eat regularly when your body is first adapting to ketosis, even if you are not hungry or you don't feel like it, so your body gets enough calories and nutrients to support it during this transition phase.

Try to get plenty of sleep: Your body may be fatigued and your mind foggy – don't aggravate those symptoms by skimping on your sleep as well. If you don't already, now is a good time to implement positive sleep habits and rituals, to ensure you're getting the rest you need.

Add more fibre to your diet: Without fruit, grains and legumes providing the fibre in your diet, your gastrointestinal system might get a little backed up. Most of us aren't getting enough fibre as it is, so reducing our fibre intake puts us way under the recommended daily amount. Address this problem by adding more keto-friendly fibre-rich foods to your diet, including leafy greens, avocado, berries and certain nuts and seeds, such as chia seeds or walnuts. You can also take a supplement to help support bowel movement (see page 48 for more information). As your body adjusts, your gastrointestinal system likely will as well.

KETO BREATH

Acetone is one of the three types of ketones that your body creates when it is in ketosis, and also one that the body expels quite a bit of, mainly through the breath. Acetone has a very distinct, somewhat unpleasant, fruity smell, which will become apparent in your breath once your body is in ketosis. Though the scent will be strong at first, along with a possible metallic taste in your mouth, it will lessen as your body adjusts to its new metabolic state.

Drink more water: Just as drinking more water can help with other symptoms of going keto, it can help lessen the unpleasant smell of keto breath as well.

Brush your teeth often: Brushing your teeth in the morning and at night might not be enough to alleviate your keto breath. Carry a travel-sized toothbrush and toothpaste with you, so you can brush as often as you like.

Chew keto-friendly gum: Chewing gum is the quickest and most convenient way to eliminate bad breath, just make sure to check the sugar and carb content before you pop it in your mouth. Look for gum that uses natural flavours and is sweetened with xylitol, or other keto-friendly sweeteners.

EFFECTS & HEALTH BENEFITS OF KETO

While the process of switching from a carb-heavy diet to a keto one might cause some temporary unpleasant symptoms, once your body has adjusted there are some very beneficial effects, which can lead to long-term health.

SHORT-TERM EFFECTS

Greater energy: In a fast-paced world where burnout and exhaustion are often par for the course, for many it is the promise of greater, more sustained energy that makes eating keto so appealing. With a carb-heavy diet, our body relies on being constantly fuelled in order to properly function. Excess sugar causes spikes in our blood glucose, followed by crashes, and this translates to our level of energy as well. When your body can consistently draw energy from its stored fat, that mid-morning or afternoon slump is essentially eliminated.

Mood stabilisation: The constant spikes and crashes of high-carb diets paired with the tendency towards overeating in the Western diet, affect not only our energy levels, but also our mood. If you have ever been 'hangry' – that feeling of irritability and impatience when you have waited too long to eat – you have an intimate understanding of the concept. With a steady and constant source of energy in the body (from stored fat as opposed to glucose), you eliminate the blood sugar rollercoaster, which also helps mitigate mood swings.

Mental clarity: Another benefit that goes hand in hand with greater energy and fewer mood swings, is the mental clarity many people feel when eating a keto diet. A high-carb diet may be the culprit of 'brain fog', or that feeling that your mind isn't firing on all cylinders. Cutting carb intake is often credited with a greater sense of alertness and ability to focus.

Clear healthy skin: Acne and other skin issues, including psoriasis and eczema, are often linked to diet, and many find that eating keto can help clear up skin and reduce flare-ups.

The alleviation of Premenstrual Syndrome (PMS): For women, eating a keto diet can contribute to the alleviation of symptoms related to the menstrual cycle. Many women find that a keto diet can help with menstrual-related cramps, acne breakouts, mood swings and cycle regulation.

LONG-TERM EFFECTS

Though research is limited, there are some studies that show eating a keto diet can help protect against age-related illnesses. Eliminating the regular glucose and insulin spikes that come with a carb-heavy diet can help prevent insulin resistance, protecting against type 2 diabetes. A keto diet also seems to boost neurovascular function, particularly in protecting against the accumulation of beta-amyloid proteins in the brain, which can lead to Alzheimer's disease.

KETO & WEIGHT LOSS

One of the main reasons the keto diet has gained so much traction in the health and wellness worlds, is due to the rather rapid and reliable weight loss that eating ketogenically can bring about. To understand this effect, it is worth taking a closer look at how the standard Western diet can contribute to weight gain in the first place.

THE SCIENCE OF WEIGHT GAIN

We already know that our body first turns to glucose when converting energy for use. Glucose comes from carbohydrates, and, though you might not realise it, there are carbohydrates in almost everything we eat – not just the obvious items, such as bread, sweets, rice and pasta, but in fruit, legumes, vegetables and even dairy (especially dairy items that are not full fat). In a diet that is made up mostly of carbohydrates, and often unhealthy ones high in sugar and bad fat, the bloodstream is inundated with glucose on a regular basis. As mentioned before, the pancreas secretes insulin in response to glucose, which then shuttles glucose to the cells for use. But the cells can only use so much glucose. Once their needs for immediate energy are met the body still has to reduce the amount of glucose in the bloodstream. Its next move is to convert glucose into glycogen, which can then be stored in the muscles and liver (see pages 10 and 16). The muscles and liver, however, can only store about a day's worth of energy (or several hours' worth of exercise). If they have reached their limited glycogen storage max, the body turns the excess glucose into fat. And there is no limit to the amount of fat that the body can store.

WHY EATING KETO REDUCES FAT

On a low-carb, medium-protein, high-fat diet, the body no longer uses glucose for energy, but uses fat instead. First it uses dietary fat – the good, healthy fats you ingest as part of the keto diet. But once your body is adept at using fat for fuel, it will also turn to body fat for energy, reducing the amount of fat (from excess glucose) that your body has been storing.

'GOOD' CARBS VS 'BAD' CARBS

Not all carbohydrates are created equal. There are many high-carb, nutrient-dense foods – such as sweet potatoes and carrots – that are healthy and provide vitamins, minerals and fibre to the body. As they contain fibre, this means that the carbs are more slowly absorbed by the body, avoiding major spikes in insulin. Their high-carb content means their intake is limited on a keto diet, but it doesn't mean that they are bad for you. It just means that eliminating them will help accelerate weight loss. Refined carbs, such as 'white' grains and added sugars, are the main culprits.

THE PROBLEM WITH SUGAR

It's not just the glucose that sweet foods dump into our system that's problematic, but it's also the way our body reacts to them. Sugar has been shown to be highly addictive, which only perpetuates our consumption, and over consumption. In fact, it's a vicious cycle. Let's start with a piece of cake. When you eat that piece of cake, your taste buds recognise that it is delicious, and it stimulates the pleasure centres in your brain. Your brain releases dopamine, the same feel-good neurotransmitter released by illicit recreational drugs, and in reaction to the high dose of glucose hitting your bloodstream, the pancreas secretes a spike of insulin. That huge spike in insulin quickly drops your blood sugar levels, and also signals to your body that it should be storing fat. Not only does that drop in blood sugar dissipate that feel-good feeling, or sugar 'high', but it also makes you feel hungry, and kickstarts your craving for more sugar, which makes the whole cycle repeat itself. Until, you break the pattern, a crucial component and outcome of the keto diet.

THE VICIOUS SUGAR CYCLE

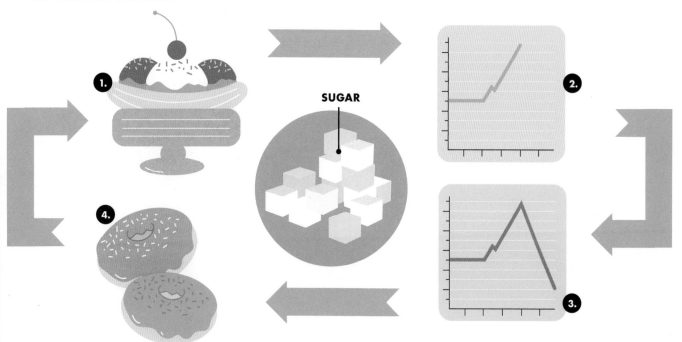

SUGAR

1. You eat sugar
You like it. You crave it. It is delicious and addictive.

2. Blood sugar spikes
Dopamine is released. Insulin is secreted to bring down blood sugar.

3. Blood sugar drops
High insulin signals fat storage. You miss the sugar 'high'.

4. Hunger & cravings
Low blood sugar increases hunger and makes you crave more sugar.

LIFESTYLE CHANGES FOR SUCCESS

Excess sugar and carbohydrates are far from the only things that contribute to weight gain. An excess of calories in general can cause weight gain, whether they come in the form of carbohydrates, fats or proteins (though fats and proteins do not perpetuate the same cycle of blood sugar spikes, drops and cravings that refined carbohydrates and sugar do). A sedentary lifestyle, poor sleep, high levels of stress and a number of other lifestyle and health factors can contribute to weight gain. Which is why eating ketogenically isn't a one-stop shop for healthfulness – it's simply a way of addressing the dietary portion of an overall healthy lifestyle.

Managing stress, as well as getting adequate sleep and plenty of exercise and movement are all crucial elements of an overall healthy lifestyle. Simply eating a keto diet is only one piece of the puzzle. In order to make your dietary switch to keto as successful as possible, you might want to take a look at other areas of your life as well. As mentioned our sleep habits, responses to stress, and whether or not we consistently move our bodies work hand in hand with our dietary choices to enhance our overall wellbeing.

SLEEP

Getting good sleep is crucial to good health. We are all familiar with the way a bad night of sleep makes us feel – mentally it makes us function at a sub-par level, and emotionally we can be subject to instability and mood swings. In terms of appetite, being tired can cause us to overeat and indulge in less than healthy foods (especially sugar), as we try to get a quick energy boost to combat fatigue. On the other hand, not only does a good night's sleep make us feel rested, but it also boosts immunity and helps our body heal.

- **Support your circadian rhythm:** Our body is programmed to wake with the rising sun and sleep after dark. Nurture this natural inclination by adjusting your sleep schedule to closer fit our ancestral rhythm.

- **Limit artificial light and electronic devices:** One of the reasons we no longer sleep and wake according to our circadian rhythm is because of electricity and artificial light, which can fake an eternal daytime. Add the bright blue light emanating from the many screens of our electronic devices – from televisions to smartphones to tablets – and our innate power to sleep deeply goes haywire. Dim the lights and go device-free an hour before bedtime to signal to your body that it's time to rest.

- **Create a bedtime ritual:** Having a nightly routine, whether it involves taking a bath or reading a book, is another way to signal to your body that it's time to rest.

- **Make your bedroom a sanctuary:** It's difficult to rest in a room that doesn't feel restful. If possible, make your bedroom a screen-free zone, keep clutter to a minimum, and invest in bedding and pillows that make you want to go to bed.

STRESS

The detrimental effects of chronic stress on our health are widely known, but with our busier, connected-24/7 modern lifestyles, our stress levels only seem to be going up, and with them our tendency to satiate heightened nerves with sweet treats and alcoholic beverages, neither of which supports a keto way of eating. Finding tools to manage stress and cultivate ways to bring down that cortisol can make a big difference in overall wellbeing.

• **Meditate regularly:** Meditation isn't for everyone, but if you can make it a regular practice the benefits are plentiful. Start with just a couple of minutes every other day and work your way up to five minutes on a daily basis. After a while, you might even find you look forward to it!

• **Keep a journal:** Journalling can be a great way to relieve some of the stress of daily life. Journalling when you start a keto diet is especially beneficial as you can record how you feel and track the changes you are going through, mentally, emotionally and physically.

• **Make room for downtime:** In a culture that values productivity above all else, it can be difficult to enjoy some quiet time to 'do nothing' by yourself without feeling guilty. But 'doing nothing' is actually a wonderful way to reset, and intentionally slow down the pace of modern life.

• **Foster real-life friendships:** We can double-tap pictures all day long on social media platforms, but it's the friendships and connections we make in real life that truly nourish us. Make those relationships a priority, cultivate a loving support network, and even the high-stress times will lose some of their intensity.

• **Get in touch with your breath:** Breath is the very thing that gives us life, yet most of us don't give it a second thought, and because of that our breathing is shallow and rather superficial, residing only in our chest and the upper portions of our lungs. Experimenting with breathwork, or breathing exercises that alter your breathing pattern with intention, can be a powerful way to ground yourself, relieve tension and increase energy.

• **Make time for regular exercise:** The mental benefits of exercise are just as undeniable as its physical advantages. It releases endorphins, which combat anxiety, and helps promote good sleep, which, as we know, in turn alleviates stress and promotes overall health. Read on for more detailed information about exercising while starting and continuing a keto diet.

KETO & EXERCISE

Physical activity plays a major role in our overall health and wellbeing. Whether you are a triathlete or just an aspiring exerciser, there are some things you should take into account when integrating exercise and the start of a keto diet.

DON'T INTRODUCE HIGH-INTENSITY EXERCISE

If you are someone who is relatively sedentary, starting a keto diet is not the time to also initiate a rigorous exercise practice. Your body will already be adapting to one major shift, and you want to make sure you make that shift successfully, rather than trying to change all of your habits at once. Wait until you've become accustomed to eating ketogenically, then introduce a well-rounded exercise routine to your daily life.

CONSIDER SCALING BACK

If you are an active person, you will probably want to consider scaling back your exercise routine during the first week or two of eating keto, when you are most likely to experience keto flu symptoms, such as fatigue, headaches and brain fog. As your body first adjusts to its new method of energy consumption, it is probably not a great idea to train for a marathon or enter a weightlifting contest.

START SLOW

In general, when starting a keto diet, low-impact, low-intensity exercise is best. Walking fits that bill perfectly so try to get out daily, whether it is to walk your dog, or simply take a sunset stroll around the block. A gentle yoga practice can also be beneficial. After a couple of weeks you can increase your rate of activity to what feels comfortable to you, but you will likely want to continue a somewhat scaled-back routine. After your body has adjusted to your new keto diet, you can return to your normal rate and regularity of exercise, just make sure to pay attention to how your body feels, and adjust your activity and/or diet in response.

MAKE SURE TO EAT ENOUGH

Because appetite suppression can be an effect of the keto diet, it is important to make sure you are eating enough to support your level of activity. Stick to meeting your macronutrient calculations (see page 40 for guidance on how to manually calculate your macronutrient needs), especially on exercise days, and you should be fine.

LISTEN TO YOUR BODY

As your body adapts to eating keto, it might also react differently to your normal workout routines, especially if they are high impact and high intensity. Pay attention to your body's signals and if you are regularly feeling dizzy or depleted, adjust your activity or diet accordingly.

EXERCISE GUIDELINES WHEN STARTING KETO

....

If you would like to implement an exercise routine while starting the keto diet, take a look at the following guidelines, which offer low-impact, low-intensity suggestions for moving your body as it adjusts to a new way of eating. Stay attuned to how your body feels and adjust the duration and intensity of your exercise routine as you see fit.

MONDAY

Take a 30-minute walk around your neighbourhood or on a treadmill.

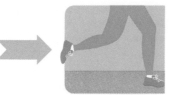

FRIDAY

Take a 30-minute walk around your neighbourhood or on a treadmill.

TUESDAY

Take a gentle yoga class or practise at home. If you don't do yoga, try some stretching exercises to boost your mobility and loosen up any tight spots.

SATURDAY

Take a gentle yoga class or practise at home. If you don't do yoga, try some stretching exercises to boost your mobility and loosen up any tight spots.

WEDNESDAY

Take a 30-minute walk around your neighbourhood or on a treadmill.

SUNDAY

Take the day off and enjoy some rest and recuperation.

THURSDAY

Engage in some lightweight training or body resistance exercises. Increase or decrease the weight and number of repetitions depending on how your body feels.

FOODS TO AVOID

So, what does a keto diet actually look like? Knowing you should avoid grains, sugar and unhealthy fat is one thing, but understanding exactly what that means, and all the ways in which we consume these things without even knowing or realising it, can be a little more difficult. Here's a closer look at the foods that you will want to eliminate altogether or eat in very limited amounts.

SUGAR

Sugar is the first thing you will want to cut from your diet when you decide to go keto, as it spikes your glucose and has no nutritional value whatsoever. This includes obvious things (like cake), but it also includes natural sweeteners too. The thing about sugar is that it is sneaky, showing up in all kinds of items under a variety of names, so be sure to check the labels on your dressings and condiments, as well as flavoured yoghurt, trail mix and anything packaged or pre-made. Avoid all sugar and treats including:

- Granulated sugar
- Raw (demerara) sugar
- High-fructose corn syrup
- Honey
- Maple syrup
- Agave
- Cake
- Cupcakes
- Cookies
- Ice cream
- Milk chocolate
- Candy

GRAINS

Because grains, yes, even whole grains, contain carbohydrates, they are not included in a keto diet. Avoid the following grains and flour-based items:

- Wheat
- Corn
- Quinoa
- Rice
- Oats
- Barley
- Buckwheat
- Pasta
- Breads
- Cereals
- Tortillas
- Chips
- Pastries
- Crackers
- Pancakes
- Waffles

LEGUMES

Legumes are often a good source of protein and fibre in a standard healthy diet, but they are high in carbohydrates, which means they should be eliminated or greatly limited. You will want to steer clear of many legumes, and legume-based items including:

- Kidney beans
- Adzuki beans
- Black beans
- Pinto beans
- White beans
- Soy beans
- Lentils
- Chickpeas (garbanzo beans)
- Hummus
- Tofu

STARCHY VEGETABLES

Though vegetables make up a large portion of a healthy keto diet, some vegetables are too high in carbs to keep the body in ketosis. A general rule of thumb to keep in mind is that vegetables that grow above ground are acceptable, while root vegetables tend to be higher in carbs. Avoid the following starchy vegetables:

- Potatoes
- Sweet potatoes
- Yams
- Corn

And limit your intake of the following starchy vegetables:

- Carrots
- Beetroot (beets)
- Peas

SUGAR

LEGUMES

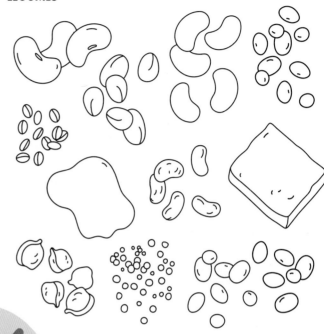

GRAINS

STARCHY VEGETABLES

FRUIT

UNHEALTHY FATS & OILS

LOW-FAT DAIRY

SWEETENED BEVERAGES

FRUIT

Fresh fruits are high in vitamins and nutrients, but they are also high in natural sugars, which means the majority of them are off limits when it comes to a keto diet. This goes for fruit in any form, whether it is fresh, dried, baked or preserved. You will want to avoid most fruits, including:

- Bananas
- Pineapple
- Apples
- Oranges
- Kiwifruit
- Mango
- Grapes
- Tangerines
- Peaches
- Pears
- Cherries
- Watermelon

LOW-FAT DAIRY

Many dairy products are reliably keto-friendly unless they are reduced fat. Without the fat, these items have too many carbohydrates to keep your body in ketosis, though even full-fat milk has more carbs than a strictly keto diet has room for. Avoid the following dairy products:

- Low-fat yoghurt
- Low-fat cheese
- Skimmed or non-fat milk

UNHEALTHY FATS & OILS

Fat is another major element in the keto diet, in fact, it's the most crucial one. But it's important to get your daily allotment from healthy fats (see page 34). Unhealthy fats are found in a number of vegetable and seed oils typically used for cooking, so be sure to steer clear of the following:

- Rapeseed oil
- Corn oil
- Grapeseed oil
- Peanut oil
- Sunflower oil
- Safflower oil

SWEETENED BEVERAGES

You might be very thirsty when you first transition to eating keto, but many beverages are off limits due to their high carb or sugar content. Avoid the following:

- Fizzy drinks
- Diet fizzy drinks
- Juice
- Kombucha
- Energy drinks
- Sweetened teas
- Sweetened coffee drinks

DRINKING ALCOHOL ON KETO

Though many items are clearly not keto-friendly, alcohol is something that falls into a grey area. Some types of alcohol, like beer, are heavy on the carbs, making them a keto no-go. And mixed drinks often feature juices, fizzy drinks and syrups that are packed with sugar, so they should also be avoided. But there are certain wines and alcohols that won't drastically up your carb intake; they will, however, affect your state of ketosis. Once alcohol is in your bloodstream, your liver will work extra hard to eliminate it, processing it before it works on turning your fatty acids into ketones, slowing your rate of ketosis.

Because you are eating a low-carb diet, your tolerance for alcohol will be lower while your susceptibility to hangovers will be higher. Being under the influence of alcohol may also make you more susceptible to consuming non-keto-friendly foods, as anyone who has eaten a 2 am slice of pizza will understand. So throwing back several shots of tequila, while technically keto-friendly, might not be the best idea. Half a glass of a nice pinot noir with dinner however, is probably fine. One of the main reasons many people switch to a keto diet is to live a healthier lifestyle in general, and that often excludes regular and excessive use of alcohol whether it's keto-friendly or not.

FOODS TO EAT: FAT

You now know what not to eat, but what should a keto diet include? Eating fat has got a bad rap, thanks to the proliferation of low-fat diets and foods that gained popularity over the past few decades. But including healthy fats in your diet has many benefits: not only does fat make food taste better and keep us satiated longer, but it also helps us absorb certain vitamins and minerals, and is crucial for cell and muscle health as well as brain function. And, as we've covered, eating fat does not lead to our body's storage of fat, as we've been made to believe; sugar and carbohydrates shoulder most of the blame when it comes to weight gain.

Fat makes up the majority of calories on a ketogenic diet, and it is what your body will use to make energy as opposed to carbohydrates. But that doesn't mean you should go on a fried food bender: just as carbs are not created equal, neither are all fats. It is imperative that your fat intake comes from healthy, mostly whole sources.

WHERE TO GET HEALTHY FATS

The best fat you can eat comes from whole foods – items that have not been altered, added to or processed. You can also find them in oils derived from fruits and vegetables. This is where you need to be discerning about which oils and fats you choose. Many oils, including most vegetable oils, are highly processed, often even extracted with the use of chemicals, which changes their make-up and eliminates their healthful effects. Look for oils that have the least amount of processing and come from the highest-quality ingredients. Butter and ghee, or clarified butter, are also good sources of fat, especially if they come from organic, pasture-raised cows.

HEALTHY FATS:

- Nuts
- Seeds
- Avocados
- Olives
- Meat
- Yoghurt
- Eggs
- Fatty fish
- Extra virgin olive oil
- Unrefined coconut oil
- Butter
- Ghee

FAT BOMBS

Fat bombs (p. 180) are like the secret weapon of convenient keto eating. Often easy to make, and tasty too, these fat-heavy snacks are comprised of ingredients that offer mostly fat (as we know, eating enough fat is the main key to keeping your body in ketosis) like coconut oil or high-fat dairy. They make great snacks or desserts, but they can also act as a meal replacement if you don't have the time (or the appetite) for a full meal. Always having fat bombs on hand is a quick, easy and tasty way to help you stick to this new and somewhat challenging way of eating, while ensuring you reach your fat intake for the day.

FOODS TO EAT: CARBOHYDRATES

Eating low carb doesn't mean no carbs. But this is the area you will need to be most attentive to. A lot of your carbs will come from fruits and vegetables, but some are more keto-friendly than others. And when eating keto, total carbs vs net carbs is an important distinction, so be sure to keep that in mind.

VEGETABLES

We don't typically think of vegetables when we think of carbs, but on a keto diet, veggies, particularly low-carb ones, are where most of your daily carb intake will come from. As we have already covered, there are a number of starchy vegetables that have more carbs than eating ketogenically has room for, and their intake should be limited. But there are lots of nutrient-dense, low-carb vegetables that you can and should enjoy. Eating a variety of these veggies will help make your meals interesting as well as ensure you get the vitamins and minerals you need for overall health.

FRUIT

As previously mentioned, because of their high natural sugar content, most fruits are not keto-friendly. There are some fruits, however, that are on the lower end of the carb scale, and can be included in your meals without putting your body out of ketosis. These include some items that are often thought of as vegetables, but actually fall into the fruit category. Blueberries and tomatoes are low carb enough to be included in a keto diet, but on the higher side of the low end so they should still be eaten in moderation.

KETO-FRIENDLY VEGETABLES:

- Leafy greens (spinach, kale and all kinds of lettuce)
- Cauliflower
- Broccoli
- Brussels sprouts
- Green beans
- Cabbage
- Asparagus
- Fennel

KETO-FRIENDLY FRUIT:

- Cucumbers
- Bell peppers (capsicums)
- Eggplants (aubergines)
- Lemons
- Limes
- Strawberries
- Blackberries
- Raspberries
- Blueberries
- Tomatoes

TOTAL CARBS VS NET CARBS

When embarking on a low-carb diet like keto, every carb counts, especially when too many can put your body out of ketosis. But when you are counting carbs, there is a big difference between total carbs and net carbs. Total carbs are just that: the total amount of carbohydrates in whatever food you are eating. Because dietary fibre, which is technically carbohydrates, has little impact on blood sugar, you can subtract the grams of dietary fibre from the number of total carbohydrate grams in order to get the 'net' carb amount, a more realistic look at the amount of carbohydrates that will have an effect on your system. Not all foods contain it, but most items made with an alternative sweetener (like xylitol or erythritol) will also have sugar alcohol content, which similarly has minimal impact on your blood sugar level and can also be subtracted from your total carb intake, allowing more room on your plate for fruit or veggies.

FOODS TO EAT: PROTEIN

While calories from fat make up the highest percentage of your dietary intake, protein is just as important for a successful foray into keto. First and foremost, protein is a crucial building block of the body – not only for hair and nails, which are mostly made of protein, but also bones, muscles, cartilage, skin and blood. Protein also helps us to feel full after a meal, and though the pancreas responds to it by secreting insulin, it doesn't trigger the production of nearly as much of it as carbohydrates do, avoiding the sugar spike of a carb-heavy meal.

Remember though, that while eating enough protein on a keto diet is necessary, particularly to prevent muscle loss, eating too much can kick your body out of ketosis.

ANIMAL VS PLANT PROTEIN

Protein can come from a number of different sources, and many sources of fat are also good sources of protein. Many animal-based items are good sources of protein. Though there are many plant-based foods high in protein, such as quinoa, lentils, tofu and beans, as mentioned these foods are also high in carbs – not good options for a keto diet.

KETO-FRIENDLY PROTEINS:

- Meat
- Poultry
- Seafood
- Eggs
- Cheese
- Yoghurt
- Nuts
- Nut butters

HIGH-QUALITY ANIMAL PROTEIN

When it comes to animal-based protein, some options are better than others. If possible, seek out organic, pasture-raised, grass-fed meat, so you know it comes from animals that lived a relatively happy, stress-reduced life, free of grain-based diets and excessive antibiotics. Sourcing your meat from a local sustainable farmer is even better, since you will know exactly where your meat came from. You will also want to opt for buying wild fish as it contains more nutrients than farmed fish, which may also be ingesting pollutants from less-than-clean fish feed. Of course, buying such high-quality meat, poultry and seafood can be cost-prohibitive, so buy the best quality that your budget allows, and don't let the possibility of high price tags put you off keto. Even if your steak isn't grass fed, it is still better for you than any sort of packaged or processed meal you might otherwise be tempted to eat.

KETO CALCULATIONS

Whereas many 'diets' involve counting calories, with keto, calculating macronutrients is the most important consideration. And while the percentages of macronutrients needed in a keto diet are relatively standard across the board, what they translate to in terms of every individual's needs will vary.

In general, 60–75% of your caloric intake should come from fat, 15–30% from protein and just 5–10% from carbs. To start, you can aim for 70% fat, 25% protein and 5% carbs, but every body is different and you might need to adjust your macros depending on your level of exercise, how you feel, and the results you see.

There are a number of online calculators available that will take into account your height, weight, sex and physical activity level. But it is possible to make this calculation manually as well.

First, you will need to calculate your basal metabolic rate (BMR), which is the basic number of calories your body needs to exist. To do this, you can use the Mifflin-St Jeor equation:

WOMEN: *10 x weight (kg) + 6.25 x height (cm) – 5 x age (y) – 161*

MEN: *10 x weight (kg) + 6.25 x height (cm) – 5 x age (y) + 5*

Next you will need to figure out your total energy expenditure, or your BMR plus the amount of calories needed depending on your level of exercise and activity.

CALCULATING YOUR ENERGY EXPENDITURE

LEVEL OF ACTIVITY:		MULTIPLY YOUR BMR BY:
Mostly sedentary	→	1.2
Lightly active (exercise 1 to 3 x per week)		1.375
Moderately active (exercise 3 to 5 x per week)	→	1.55
Heavily active (near daily exercise)		1.725
Extremely active (multiple workouts per day)	→	1.9

FOR EXAMPLE

To find the BMR of a 30-year-old woman who is 158.5 cm (5 ft 2 in) tall and weighs 55.7 kg (125 lb), the equation would look like this:

10 x 55.7 (kg) + 6.25 x 158.5 (cm) – 5 x 30 – 161

For a total BMR of 1236. If she is lightly active, her BMR is multiplied by 1.375 for a total daily caloric intake of about 1700.

To find the BMR of a 35-year-old man who is 175.26 cm (5 ft 9 in) and weighs 79.38 kg (175 lb), the equation would look like this:

10 x 79.38 (kg) + 6.25 x 175.26 (cm) – 5 x 35 + 5

For a total BMR of 1738. If he is moderately active, his BMR is multiplied by 1.55 for a total daily caloric intake of about 2700.

CALCULATING YOUR MACRONUTRIENTS

Once you have your total daily calorie intake, you can calculate how much of each macronutrient you will need, using the general ketogenic percentages.

Protein: Protein will make up 25% of your diet. To calculate how many grams of protein you will need in a day, complete the following sum:
daily caloric intake x .25 ÷ 4*
*as protein contains 4 calories per gram

Fat: Fat will make up 70% of your diet. To calculate how many grams of fat you will need in a day, complete the following sum:
daily caloric intake x .70 ÷ 9*
*as fat contains 9 calories per gram

Carbohydrates: Your remaining calories will come from carbohydrates. To calculate how many grams of carbohydrates you can have in a day, complete the following sum:
daily caloric intake x .05 ÷ 4*
*as carbohydrates contain 4 calories per gram
The resulting number is how many grams of carbs you should eat in a day. Remember, this number reflects net carbs (total carbs – dietary fibre), as covered on page 36. As a general rule of thumb, you will want to aim for eating 20–25 g of carbs in a day.

FOR EXAMPLE

For the woman whose daily caloric intake is about 1700, her macronutrient breakdown looks like this: 106 g protein, 132 g fat, 21 g carbs. For the man whose daily caloric intake is about 2700, his macronutrient breakdown looks like this: 169 g protein, 210 g fat, 33 g carbs. Though these percentages are a good place to start, everyone is different, so you might need to fine-tune your ratios. You may also want to adjust your macronutrients intake if your average level of exercise increases or decreases. And as your body changes after a period of eating ketogenically, it's worth recalculating your macronutrients.

TRACKING YOUR MACRONUTRIENTS

For someone who is not used to tracking what they eat, monitoring every meal and snack may feel overwhelming. Since limiting carbohydrates is the most crucial element of a keto diet, you can ease into the process by calculating your daily carb intake, while generally making sure you eat enough protein and plenty of fat. When you're ready to start diligently tracking your intake, you'll probably find it helpful to use a food-tracking app where you can input your macronutrient needs, find out the macronutrient make-up of specific foods, and see your progress.

KETO-FRIENDLY SWAPS

....

There are lots of keto-friendly alternatives to many diet staples, from swapping zucchini (courgettes) for pasta to replacing flour with ground nuts. Here are some common swaps.

SPAGHETTI
Per serving: 221 cals / 1.3 g fat / 43 g carbs / 2.5 g fibre / 40.5 g net carbs / 9 g protein / Serving size 200 g (7 oz)

ZOODLES (P. 68)
Per serving: 19 cals / 0.4 g fat / 3.5 g carbs / 1.1 g fibre / 2.4 g net carbs / 1.4 g protein / Serving size 200 g (7 oz)

WHITE RICE
Per serving: 206 cals / 0.4 g fat / 45 g carbs / 1.6 g fibre / 43.4 g net carbs / 4.3 g protein / Serving size 150 g (5½ oz)

CAULI-RICE (P. 72)
Per serving: 20 cals / 0 g fat / 4 g carbs / 2 g fibre / 2 g net carbs / 2 g protein / Serving size 150 g (5½ oz)

GRANULATED SUGAR
Per serving: 16 cals / 0 g fat / 4.2 g carbs / 0 g fibre /
4.2 g net carbs / 0 g protein / Serving size 4 g (⅛ oz)

ERYTHRITOL
Per serving: 0 cals / 0 g fat / 4 g carbs / 0 g fibre / 4 g net carbs /
0 g protein / Serving size 4 g (⅛ oz)

PANCAKE
Per serving: 175 cals / 7 g fat / 22.1 g carbs / 0 g fibre /
22.1 g net carbs / 5.2 g protein / Serving size 77 g (2¾ oz)

KETO PANCAKE (P. 88)
Per serving: 220 cals / 18 g fat / 7.6 g carbs / 3.7 g fibre /
3.9 g net carbs / 7 g protein / Serving size 77 g (2¾ oz)

PINEAPPLE
Per serving: 50 cals / 0.1 g fat / 13 g carbs / 1.4 g fibre / 11.6 g net carbs / 0.5 g protein / Serving size 100 g (3½ oz)

BLACKBERRIES/RASPBERRIES
Per serving: 47.5 cals / 0.6 g fat / 10.8 g carbs / 5.9 g fibre / 4.9 g net carbs / 1.3 g protein / Serving size 100 g (3½ oz)

PLAIN (ALL-PURPOSE) FLOUR
Per serving: 364 cals / 1 g fat / 76 g carbs / 2.7 g fibre / 73.3 g net carbs / 10 g protein / Serving size 100 g (3½ oz)

ALMOND FLOUR
Per serving: 573.2 cals / 50.3 g fat / 19.6 g carbs / 10.8 g fibre / 8.8 g net carbs / 20.9 g protein / Serving size 100 g (3½ oz)

MILK CHOCOLATE
Per serving: 535 cals / 30 g fat / 59 g carbs / 3.4 g fibre / 55.6 g net carbs / 8 g protein / Serving size 100 g (3½ oz)

DARK CHOCOLATE
Per serving: 575 cals / 46 g fat / 27 g carbs / 10 g fibre / 17 g net carbs / 6 g protein / Serving size 100 g (3½ oz)

CASHEWS
Per serving: 553 cals / 44 g fat / 30 g carbs / 3.3 g fibre / 26.7 g net carbs / 18 g protein / Serving size 100 g (3½ oz)

MACADAMIA NUTS
Per serving: 718 cals / 76 g fat / 14 g carbs / 9 g fibre / 5 g net carbs / 8 g protein/ Serving size 100 g (3½ oz)

TOMATO KETCHUP
Per serving: 15 cals / 0 g fat / 4.1 g carbs / 0 g fibre /
4.1 g net carbs / 0.2 g protein / Serving size 15 g (½ oz, 1 tablespoon)

SMOKY TOMATO JAM (P. 74)
Per serving: 3.7 cals / 0 g fat / 1.3 g carbs / 0.2 g fibre /
1.1 g net carbs / 0.1 g protein / Serving size 15 g (½ oz, 1 tablespoon)

MAYONNAISE
Per serving: 93.5 cals / 10.3 g fat / 0.1 g carbs / 0 g fibre /
0.1 g net carbs / 0.1 g protein / Serving size 15 g (½ oz, 1 tablespoon)

AVOCADO OIL MAYO (P. 74)
Per serving: 112 cals / 12.5 g fat / 0.1 g carbs / 0 g fibre /
0.1 g net carbs / 0.2 g protein / Serving size 15 g (½ oz, 1 tablespoon)

WHOLEMEAL (WHOLE-WHEAT) BREAD
Per serving: 138.6 cals / 1.9 g fat / 23.5 g carbs / 3.3 g fibre / 20.2 g net carbs / 6.8 g protein / Serving size 55 g (2 oz, 1 thick slice)

SEEDED KETO BREAD (P. 84)
Per serving: 266.8 cals / 22.6 g fat / 11.5 g carbs / 7 g fibre / 4.5 g net carbs / 7.6 g protein / Serving size 55 g (2 oz)

PORRIDGE
Per serving: 307 cals / 5.3 g fat / 54.8 g carbs / 8.2 g fibre / 46.6 g net carbs / 10.7 g protein / Serving size 80 g (2¾ oz)

KETO 'OAT' MEAL (P. 86)
Per serving: 356.9 cals / 29.7 g fat / 10.8 g carbs / 7.2 g fibre / 3.6 g net carbs / 12.9 g protein / Serving size 113 g (4 oz)

SUPPLEMENTING KETO

While eating a well-balanced keto diet can provide all the nutrients and minerals the body needs, individuals can react differently to this change in eating style and many people find it helpful to add certain supplements to their diet, especially when transitioning to eating keto. Tune in to the way your body feels, and experiment with supplements you think will benefit you most. As with all dietary supplements, consult your medical practitioner before taking, seek out the highest-quality, sustainably sourced products and follow each supplement's particular dosage and intake instructions.

SUPPLEMENTS TO CONSIDER

Magnesium: Magnesium is an important electrolyte, one that helps regulate blood glucose levels, boosts energy and supports immunity. Because you lose a lot of electrolytes when switching to a low-carb way of eating, it might be helpful to take a magnesium supplement. Magnesium also promotes muscle relaxation and sleep, so consider taking it at night to help combat sleep disruption caused by keto 'flu' (p. 20).

Potassium: Potassium is another electrolyte that can be depleted during the dietary shift to ketosis. Potassium helps regulate fluid levels in the body, which keeps us hydrated, and also supports the nervous system, helping to maintain nerve function and regulate muscle contractions.

Psyllium: As your body adjusts to a keto diet, you might experience constipation. Adding fibre-rich vegetables can help, but supplementing with psyllium, a carb-free fibre derived from the seeds of a herb called *Plantago ovata*, can act as a gentle laxative, promoting regularity as your body recalibrates.

MCT oil: MCT is an initialism for medium-chain triglycerides, easily digested fatty acids that do not need to be broken down by the body, which can be used immediately for energy and are believed to help increase ketone production. Supplementing your diet with MCT oil (available in powdered and liquid form), especially in the early days, can help up your ketone production and perhaps ease some symptoms of the keto 'flu'. It is also a useful cooking ingredient and appears in many of the recipes in this book.

Protein powders: The keto diet isn't high in protein, but you do need a moderate amount, and if you are pescetarian, vegetarian or simply want to limit your meat intake, a protein powder can be an easy way to help meet your daily protein requirement. Because many protein powders contain carbs, look for one that is keto-friendly.

SETTING YOURSELF UP FOR KETO SUCCESS

Eating ketogenically can feel a bit overwhelming at first, especially if you are used to eating a carb-heavy diet, and it takes a certain level of commitment in order to keep your body in ketosis. A busy schedule, eating out, travelling and social gatherings can all feel like obstacles when you are eating keto, and when you are just beginning the process, they can be enough to derail you if you don't think ahead. Here are some tips for staying on track, and facing possible obstacles with a game plan for success.

TIPS FOR STICKING TO KETO

Plan and prep your meals. Eating a keto diet on the fly isn't very practical or sustainable. In order to get the proper balance of carbs to fats to proteins in the most healthy way possible, you will want to map out your meals and snacks for the day, week or even month and prep as much as possible beforehand.

Cut food prep corners. It is OK to buy cauliflower that's already been riced, zucchini (courgettes) that have been noodled (zoodles) or any other veggies that come pre-shredded or chopped. You don't have to do it all! And you don't have to buy everything fresh, either. Sometimes it is hard to get to the farmers' market or supermarket, so keeping some items stocked in your freezer can ensure you always have keto-friendly veggies on hand.

Stay simple. The key to making keto a sustainable way of eating is to keep things simple. You shouldn't have to spend all your free time calculating macronutrients, prepping food and making complicated meals. Stick to delicious basics and the simple recipes outlined in this book for your foray into keto, and feel free to save the more labour-intensive meals for when you are more accustomed to this way of eating.

Avoid convenience foods. Most on-the-go food options are not keto-friendly, whether you are looking for a fast, inexpensive meal, or a snack from a vending machine. Just consider those options off the table and understand that you will have to plan for eating outside the home by packing your own food.

Always have snacks handy. Having ready-to-eat, keto-friendly snacks on hand at all times will help keep you on track, especially if hunger strikes when you don't yet have a meal prepared, or if you are on the go longer than you expected. Being able to snack on a handful of macadamia nuts in your bag or a stash of olives (both keto-friendly items!) in your fridge will keep you satiated until you can prepare something more to eat.

Have a handful of go-to recipes. Though meal planning and prepping are key to sustaining a keto diet, at least until this type of eating becomes second nature, it is not always possible. For those times when life gets especially busy, have a few simple, easy-to-remember keto-friendly recipes that you can whip up quickly with items you typically have on hand and some pantry staples.

Give yourself some leeway: If you are constantly stressed about what and how much you are eating, keeping to a keto diet won't be enjoyable or sustainable. Don't beat yourself up if you add some sugar to your coffee one morning, or eat a few extra raspberries for dessert in the evening. You are eating to boost your health and make your body feel good, and sometimes that means allowing yourself a little bit of flexibility.

EATING OUT

If your current lifestyle involves lunches with co-workers, dinners out and going to parties at the homes of family or friends, eating keto can at first seem like it will put a real dampener on your social life. But you don't have to avoid eating out; you just have to do so thoughtfully and with more preparation than you are probably accustomed to. Here are some strategies for keeping keto whether you are taking a client to dinner or sharing a meal with friends.

Eating at a restaurant: If you know where you will be eating out, read through the establishment's menu ahead of time and choose a few items or dishes you know will work for your diet.

If asking your waiter a lot of questions in front of your dinner date makes you feel self-conscious, call the restaurant ahead of time to ask about particular ingredients or find out their policy about substitutions.

Be wary of sauces and condiments, as they are often made with sugar and/or flour.

Instead of pre-made salad dressing, ask for olive oil with lemon, vinegar or blue cheese.

Add healthy fats to dishes by asking for extra olive oil, butter or avocado on the side.

Eating at a friend's: If you plan on going to dinner at a friend's house, ask ahead of time what they plan on serving, and offer to bring a dish or two to add to the spread. That way you can ensure there will be at least something keto-friendly for you to eat.

Snack on something keto-friendly at home before you leave, so you are not famished when you arrive, and tempted to resort to the food being served that doesn't fit with your diet.

Consider being flexible. If eating strictly keto while enjoying the company and graciousness of friends or relatives feels stressful or takes the fun out of the evening, allow yourself to choose minor indulgences and remember that it is only one meal – you can eat as strictly keto as you like when preparing your own food at home.

DIFFERENT APPROACHES TO EATING KETO

The main guidelines of eating a keto diet – low carbs, medium protein and high fat in order to promote a state of nutritional ketosis – are standard, but there are different ways to approach it. You may be wondering whether to stick with keto short term or long term, and what that even means. For some, you may be wondering if eating keto is compatible with a vegetarian or vegan diet, all of which we will touch on here.

SHORT TERM VS LONG TERM

Because of keto's rise in popularity, it has the reputation of a fad diet. But as we have established, it is not a quick-fix kind of dietary change. It takes quite a bit of planning and commitment, and even some trial and error, to get to (and stay in) your optimal state of ketosis. But for interested people who are willing to make big lifestyle changes, and healthfully shift their way of eating, there is one question that often arises: How long should the keto diet last?

The answer is obviously a personal one. But there are some things to take into consideration. When it comes to keto, the phrase 'short term' is relative. As it takes quite a bit of time to prep your fridge and pantry for eating keto and to shift yourself away from carb-dependency, as well as the fact that it may take weeks to even get to a state of ketosis, you will want to decide for yourself what 'short term' actually means. This book will walk you through the first 28 days, which we recommend you wholly commit to. And though you will likely start to see results within that timeframe, the benefits will only become greater as you find the right individual balance of fat, carbs and protein, as your body adapts, and as eating ketogenically becomes less calculated and more intuitive. Many experts recommend committing to the keto diet for at least three months, to truly see its effects.

For some proponents, once they go keto they don't go back, maintaining the diet for years on end. However, while we know that a diet extremely low in fat while also high in carbs and sugar can cause a multitude of health problems over a lifetime, there is not much research into the long-term effects of eating keto, and medical practitioners have varying opinions on whether a strict keto diet should be adhered to indefinitely. If you decide to continue eating keto for the long term, do your research and talk to your medical practitioner about it.

VEGAN

For those who eat a vegan diet, excluding all animal products, going keto can be difficult to adhere to. Eliminating carbs from your diet in addition to animal products (such as meat, fish and dairy) becomes incredibly restrictive. It can also be difficult to get the right balance of carbs to protein to fats, since many plant-based sources of protein – such as tofu, tempeh and lentils – are high in carbs, leaving less room on your plate for low-carb vegetables. Vegans who go keto might also need to add more supplements to their diet, to make sure they are getting the necessary nutrients. That said, it is not impossible to go keto as a vegan, but it is likely not recommended. If veganism is important to you, you might want to reconsider adding keto restrictions to your diet as well.

VEGETARIAN

Though eating a vegetarian diet is less restrictive than eating vegan, since most vegetarians include dairy products and eggs in their diet, it can still be difficult to follow a strict keto diet, simply because it greatly narrows the variety and types of food you can enjoy. But, it isn't impossible. Good vegetarian sources of protein include nut butters, cheese, eggs and yoghurt. If you do decide to try a vegetarian keto diet, just be aware of your micronutrient intake as well, to ensure you are getting everything you need for a healthy, well-rounded diet.

KETO & FASTING

Intermittent fasting is an eating trend that taps into some of the same principles as a keto diet, and many people who eat keto also experiment with intermittent fasting, i.e., short windows of time where they abstain from eating. Eating keto essentially causes the body to mimic a state of fasting, using fat for fuel instead of a constant intake of glucose from carbohydrates – the metabolic response is basically the same, but the method is different. It is thought that intermittent fasting can put your body into ketosis more quickly, and amplify weight loss as well.

WHAT IS A FASTED STATE?

It typically takes 8–12 hours for our body to fully finish absorbing a meal. Once that meal is processed, if you haven't eaten anything since, the body enters a fasted state, and begins burning fat instead of glucose.

One of the effects of eating keto is appetite suppression. Because eating a low-carb, high-fat diet eliminates the need for glucose as a main source of energy, and can instead burn stored fat, your body can still derive energy without needing to eat food. This natural appetite suppression lends itself to intermittent fasting.

EXPERIMENTING WITH INTERMITTENT FASTING

Choose your method. There are three main methods of intermittent fasting: abstaining from food for a certain amount of time in one day, majorly restricting calories for two days in a row, or fasting for an entire 24-hour period one or two days within a week. One of the most common methods of intermittent fasting while doing keto, is to restrict eating to an 8-hour window in a day – for example, having breakfast at 10 am, and eating the last meal or snack of the day at 6 pm – so that, including overnight, you are fasting for 16 hours.

Listen to your body. Fasting isn't for everybody, but if you are interested in trying it, do your research and choose the method that best suits your needs. You might want to wait until you have your healthy ketogenic diet completely dialled in before adding another dietary restriction. Then pay attention to how your body feels, and let that inform whether or not you want to continue experimenting with it.

Stay hydrated. If you do try intermittent fasting, it is imperative that you stay hydrated during the times you are abstaining from food. Drinking water can also help with hunger during fasting, so be sure to drink plenty of it.

KETO PANTRY

Replacing your non-keto-compliant pantry ingredients with the items you will be using on a regular basis will not only help ease your transition to making low-carb, high-fat meals, it will also make your weekly shopping trips less burdensome and more efficient.

ITEMS TO STOCK UP ON

Nuts: Nuts are a great way to get protein and fat into a meal, and they are used liberally throughout these recipes, sprinkled over breakfasts, on top of salads and in many of the snacks. Stock up on low-carb, high-fat nuts such as macadamias, almonds, walnuts, brazil nuts and pine nuts.

Seeds: Like nuts, seeds are tiny nutrient-dense, fat-and-protein powerhouses that are easy to include in and sprinkle on top of many dishes. You will want to have hemp, linseed (flax), chia and pumpkin seeds on hand, as well as toasted sesame seeds.

Spices: Spices are a wonderful way to add flavour and depth to keto-friendly meals, and while they are not considered a free-for-all because they do contain carbs, a little bit can go a long way. Make sure your spice rack contains ground cumin, ground coriander, smoked paprika, cinnamon, turmeric and curry powder.

Oils: Oils are one of the most important ways of upping your fat intake, just remember to seek out the highest-quality, least-processed versions of the following: avocado oil, coconut oil, extra virgin olive oil and toasted sesame oil.

Flours & ground nuts: Since traditional wheat flour has far too many carbs for a keto-friendly diet, you will want to have alternatives on hand, including ground nuts and seeds, almond flour and coconut flour.

Vinegars: With such fat-heavy meals, vinegar plays a crucial role in adding the bright flavour of something acidic to many dishes and dressings. Apple cider vinegar is a good one to have on hand.

Ghee: Ghee, or clarified butter, is another great source of fat, and incredibly useful for cooking as well. Look for organic, grass-fed ghee.

Sweetener: Because sugar is off limits, any type of sweetener used must be carb-free and keto-friendly. Sukrin gold, monkfruit 1:1 and erythritol are some of the most common keto sweeteners.

Tinned items: Having a few tinned items stocked in your pantry will make your weekly shopping easier (and lighter). The recipes in this book regularly call for full-fat coconut milk, tinned tomatoes and passata (pureed tomatoes).

Coffee &/or matcha: Keto doesn't mean giving up your daily cup of coffee, as long as you prepare it with some added fat. If you are not a coffee drinker, matcha tea is a good beverage to have; just be sure to whisk up a keto-friendly version.

Tahini: This sesame seed paste is great for adding fat to dressings and dips.

Dried coconut: Thanks to its high fat content, coconut is a versatile keto ingredient. Keep your favourite dried coconut on hand, whether in grated, flaked or shredded form, for topping breakfast items or adding to snacks and fat bombs.

Anchovies in oil: These tiny fish pack a big punch when it comes to flavour and omega-3 fatty acids. They can be added to dressings, sauces and other dishes as well.

Stock: Stock is the base for many keto-friendly dishes including soups and stews. A cup of stock or bouillon on its own also makes a great snack, especially when you first start eating keto. Keep a stash of your favourite kind, just be sure it is low carb.

KETO-FRIENDLY FRUITS & VEGETABLES

Unlike pantry items, fruits and vegetables must be purchased on a regular basis to ensure freshness, but what follows is a list of items that are used throughout this book, so having them on hand is probably a good idea.

ITEMS TO STOCK UP ON

Raspberries & blackberries: Most fruits are off limits when eating keto, but by comparison raspberries and blackberries are incredibly low carb and nutrient-dense. They are great for adding a healthy hint of sweetness to breakfast dishes and smoothies.

Lemons & limes: Lemons and limes are the lowest-carb citrus available, and are often used to add some flavourful zest to salads and other savoury dishes. Their acidity adds a great balance to keto's high fat content.

Zucchini (courgettes): These are high in fibre – helpful for bringing down net carbs – as well as vitamins and minerals. If you have a spiraliser or mandoline, zucchini can be used to make the perfect keto alternative to noodles (p. 68).

Cauliflower: Cauliflower is another high-fibre vegetable that is also high in antioxidants. It can be used to make many alternative, keto-friendly dishes like cauliflower rice (p. 72) and crusts.

Onions: Onions are relatively low carb compared to other root vegetables and are a staple vegetable for adding flavour to savoury meals and snacks. Keep red onions and spring onions (scallions) on hand.

Garlic: Garlic is another relatively low-carb root that really packs a flavour punch – just a clove or two adds incredible taste to a number of dressings, sauces and savoury dishes.

Ginger: This low-carb root is great for spicing up dishes, and contains a number of vitamins and minerals as well.

Avocado: Avocados are keto superstars – high in healthy fats and incredibly tasty, they are basically a self-contained fat bomb.

Tomatoes: You won't want to eat too many tomatoes because of their carb content, but in limited quantity they are great for adding a bright, fresh flavour to many dishes.

Cucumbers: This low-carb fruit adds a refreshing taste and texture to salads and alternative noodle dishes.

Herbs: Like spices, herbs aren't a total free-for-all on the keto diet because their carb content can add up, but they add wonderful low-carb freshness and flavour to many savoury dishes. Keep dill, coriander (cilantro), parsley, oregano, basil and any of your other favourites stocked in your kitchen.

KETO-FRIENDLY DAIRY & PROTEINS

....

Dairy products and proteins also need to be purchased with regularity, and used rather quickly. These are the items that make repeated appearances throughout the recipes in this book, so are worth stocking up on.

ITEMS TO STOCK UP ON

Yoghurt: This is great for quick weekday breakfasts since it has a good amount of fat and protein. Some yoghurts can be high in carbs though, so be sure to buy natural full-fat Greek yoghurt or a low-carb dairy-alternative yoghurt.

Eggs: Eggs are low in carbs and not too high in protein – a very keto-friendly ratio. Plus they are very satiating; great for savoury weekend breakfasts.

Alternative milk: Dairy milk, even full-fat dairy milk, can be high in carbs. Keep your favourite alternative milk, such as almond or coconut, on hand for smoothies and golden milk (p. 90). Just make sure it is plain and unsweetened.

Double (heavy) cream: Unlike milk, thick cream is low in carbs and contains lots of fat. It is a must for adding to your morning coffee and is great in dressings and fat bombs (p. 180) too.

Buttermilk: Buttermilk is another dairy item that is low in carbs, adding lots of flavour and fat to dressings.

Cheeses: In general, cheese contains healthy amounts of protein and calcium, and is low in carbs and high in fat, making every type keto-friendly (as long as it is full fat). Stock up on parmesan, pecorino, gruyere and blue cheeses.

Beef: Beef is a high-quality source of protein and contains zero carbs. It is also very satiating. Look for organic, grass-fed meat.

Pork: Pork is another meat that can be high in fat and adds a lot of flavour to savoury dishes.

Chicken: Poultry also has no carbs and chicken is a versatile ingredient for lunch and dinners. It is also a good source of protein as long as it is paired with ample amounts of fat.

Fish: Fish is an ideal keto food, as it contains little to no carbs, ample protein and can be high in fat (particularly omega-3 fatty acids) if you purchase the right kind. Look for wild-caught salmon or cod.

Prawns (shrimp): Prawns are a keto-friendly low-carb shellfish that offer tasty variety and a good source of protein.

SPECIAL EQUIPMENT

It is possible to eat a keto diet without any special equipment, but for some of the recipes in this book, you will find that the prep and making of the meal will be much easier and more efficient with specific items or appliances. If you do not have something on this list, don't be deterred, there is certainly a workaround, it just might take a little more effort.

HELPFUL ITEMS

Muslin (cheesecloth): If you're not familiar with open-weave muslin, you will probably find you have more uses for it than you know. For the purposes of this book, muslin comes in very handy when removing the moisture from cauliflower rice, one of the basic recipes you will repeatedly be using. (A nut bag used for making nut milks, can serve the same purpose.)

Steamer insert: You will need a steamer to make cauliflower rice, a staple of most keto-friendly diets.

Baking tray: A baking tray, about 23 x 33 cm (9 x 13 in), is helpful for roasting smaller quantities of an item. Having multiple baking trays allows you to simultaneously roast various items and pull them out at different times.

Baking tin: This is one piece of kitchenware that you will likely want to invest in. It is necessary for roasting proteins and vegetables, of which you will be doing quite a bit. It is also necessary for baking snacks such as granola and trail mix.

Spiraliser or mandoline slicer: A spiraliser is a specific tool for creating 'zoodles' – noodle-like shapes cut from vegetables such as squash and zucchini (courgettes). If you already have a stand mixer, many have spiralising attachments available, but the same effect can be achieved with a less cost-prohibitive mandoline slicer.

High-powered blender: In order to make the smoothies, dressings and sauces featured, you will need a high-powered blender for easier prepping and smooth consistencies.

Food processor: A food processor will come in handy when making basic recipes like cauliflower rice and cauliflower crusts, as well as a number of the fat bombs featured in the snacks section.

Loaf (bar) tin: You will most probably already have a loaf tin in your cupboard, which will come in handy when making seeded keto bread. If not, this is another piece of kitchenware you will get a lot of use from.

Reusable jars and containers: Because you will be doing so much prep work for each week of meals, you will want to have plenty of reusable containers of various sizes for storing your prepped food as well as for storing snacks and leftovers.

28 DAYS OF EATING KETO

Now that you have the information and tools to understand how to go keto and why you might want to, it is time for the fun part – actually trying it. This section of the book will walk you through your first 28 days of eating keto, with delicious recipes for basic staples and everyday items, snacks and drinks, as well as three meals a day for the next four weeks.

RECIPES FOR KETO-FRIENDLY BASICS

Basics are just that – items that you will be using in multiple meals, whether they lay the foundation of a dish, like cauliflower rice and zucchini (courgette) noodles (zoodles), or are replacements for non-keto-friendly condiments, such as avocado oil mayonnaise and tomato jam. This is also where you will find recipes for the dressings, spice blends, sauces and pestos used throughout the 28 days of meals.

Bread is off limits, but you will find a keto version in this chapter that's packed with high-fat, nutrient-dense nuts and seeds, as well as keto versions of oatmeal and pancakes that make reliable breakfast dishes.

For many people, daily morning coffee or matcha is a basic so you will find keto-friendly versions of those in this section as well.

SAVE TIME

Make ahead: Prepping and planning are a big part of successfully going keto, and basics are a great place to get ahead in that department. Sauces and condiments can be made ahead of time, to make your daily meal prep less burdensome. The dry goods used for keto versions of oatmeal and pancakes can be pre-measured and batched to save time in the morning when making breakfast. And items such as cauliflower rice, keto bread and keto pancakes can be made ahead of time and frozen – just defrost and warm them up when you are ready to eat.

Buy prepared: Because of the rise in popularity of eating low carb and keto, there are many keto items that you can find already prepared, if not at your local supermarket then from an online health foods purveyor – you don't have to make every dish from scratch! Feel free to save yourself time (and perhaps some sanity) by buying pre-made ingredients such as keto-specific tomato ketchup and mayonnaise, as well as cauliflower that has already been riced, or made into a crust (just check the ingredients label for any hidden carbs or sugars).

ZOODLES HOW-TO

You can make zoodles (zucchini/courgette) noodles in multiples of ways — the easiest is using a worktop spiraliser or a hand-held spiraliser. If buying special equipment is not something you want to do you can use a julienne peeler, mandoline or a knife.

Spiraliser method

PREP
5 minutes

1 zucchini (courgette)

01 Create zoodles according to the spiraliser instructions, but a good tip is to use a large and thicker zucchini.

Mandoline/ knife method

PREP
5 minutes

1 zucchini (courgette)

01 Slice 5 mm (¼ in) thick slices of zucchini with a mandoline or sharp knife. Slice strips again into 5 mm thick strips.

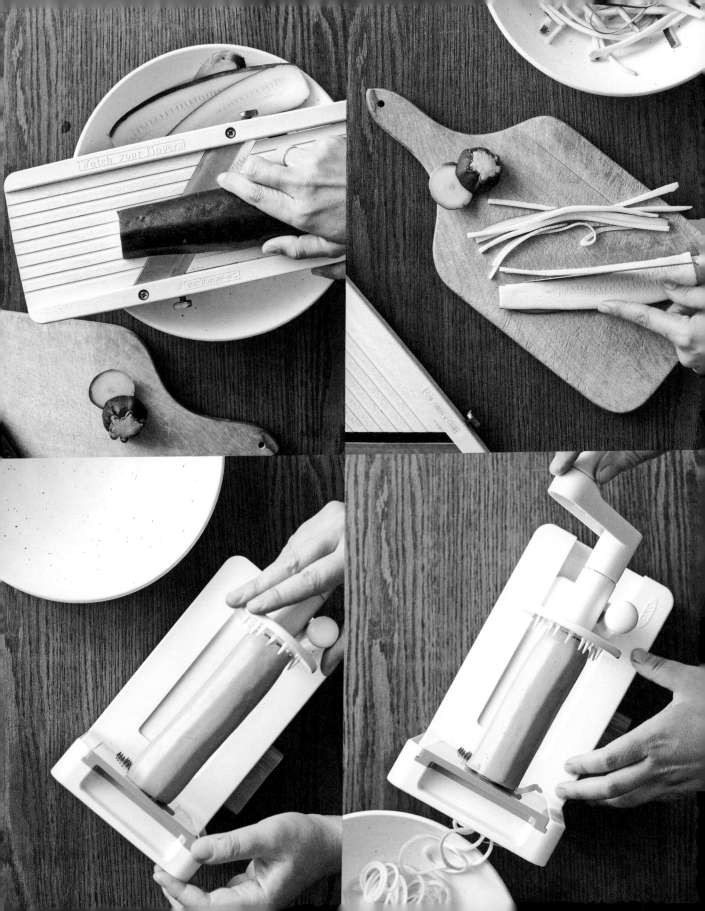

ZOODLES

....

The carb limitations of a keto diet allow no room for standard pasta, but with a little know-how, zucchini (courgettes) can be transformed into delicious noodle-like shapes, for a nutrient-dense base that won't knock you out of ketosis.

Pan method:

SERVINGS: 4
PREP / COOK TIME
15–30 minutes / 2–3 minutes

4 zucchini (courgettes)
1 teaspoon salt
½ teaspoon olive oil

01 After creating zoodles (p. 68), toss them in a colander with the salt. Leave to stand for 30 minutes, then gently squeeze zoodles to remove excess moisture (they don't have to be completely dry). Pan-fry zoodles in a non-stick frying pan with the oil for 2–3 minutes, taking care not to overcook.

Nutrition per serving:
19 cals / 4 g fat / 3.5 g carbs /
1.1 g fibre / 2.4 g net carbs /
1.4 g protein

Oven method:

SERVINGS: 4
PREP / COOK TIME
15–30 minutes / 10–15 minutes

4 zucchini (courgettes)
1 teaspoon salt

01 Preheat oven to 180°C (350°F). After creating zoodles (p. 68), toss them with the salt on a lined baking tray in an even layer, being careful not to overcrowd. Bake in the oven for 10–15 minutes.

Nutrition per serving:
19 cals / 4 g fat / 3.5 g carbs /
1.1 g fibre / 2.4 g net carbs /
1.4 g protein

ESSENTIAL ELEMENTS

These are recipes you will use repeatedly throughout the 28 days of eating keto. Cauli-rice is a great grain alternative, while the pickling liquid and roasted garlic add lots of low-carb flavour. Ground nuts can often replace flour, adding protein as well as fat to a dish.

Cauli-rice

PREP / COOK TIME

15 minutes / 0 minutes

1 whole cauliflower (about 900 g–1.4 kg/2–3 lb 1 oz)

01 Chop florets off cauliflower, place in a food processor and pulse until florets are the size of rice grains. Alternatively, chop florets until they are the size of rice grains.

Pickling liquid

PREP / COOK TIME

5 minutes / 0 minutes

250 ml (1 cup) apple cider vinegar
1 teaspoon salt
1 tablespoon sukrin gold

01 Combine ingredients with 250 ml (1 cup) of water and stir until the sukrin is dissolved.

Roasted garlic

PREP / COOK TIME

5 minutes / 45–60 minutes

1 garlic bulb
1 teaspoon olive oil
salt and pepper

01 Preheat oven to 200°C (400°F). Cut off top third of garlic bulb and discard. Place garlic in foil, drizzle with oil and season. Wrap foil around garlic and roast in oven for 45 minutes, or until cloves are lightly browned and tender.

Ground nuts

PREP / COOK TIME

5 minutes / 0 minutes

keto-friendly nuts of choice

01 Place nuts in a food processor or high-powered blender and blend until desired texture.

ROASTED
GARLIC

GROUND
NUTS

PICKLING
LIQUID

CAULI-RICE

SAUCES, CONDIMENTS & EXTRAS

Many fridge staples, such as mayonnaise and tomato ketchup, and bottled sauces and dressings include hidden sugars or unhealthy oils. These delicious substitutes and alternatives are keto-friendly and far tastier than their pre-made counterparts.

Avocado oil mayo

MAKES: 200 ML (7 FL OZ)
SERVING SIZE:
1 TABLESPOON
PREP / COOK TIME
15 minutes / 0 minutes

2 large egg yolks
  (at room temperature)
1 teaspoon Dijon mustard
1 teaspoon salt
240 ml (8 fl oz) avocado oil
1½ teaspoons apple cider
  vinegar

01 Blend yolks, mustard and salt in a high-powered blender until thick and creamy. While blending, add 60 ml (¼ cup) of oil, drop by drop, until mixture begins to thicken, then add vinegar in a slow, steady stream, followed by remaining oil. Blend until thick. Add more salt, to taste. Chill for a week.

Nutrition per serving:
136 cals / 14 g fat / 3 g carbs /
0 g fibre / 3 g net carbs /
0 g protein

Smoky tomato jam

MAKES: 250 ML (1 CUP)
SERVING SIZE:
1 TABLESPOON
PREP / COOK TIME
15 minutes / 2 hours

2 tablespoons extra virgin
  olive oil
1 large onion, chopped
450 g (1 lb) tomatoes,
  chopped
2 tablespoons monkfruit
  sweetener
1 tablespoon cider vinegar
1 teaspoon sea salt
½ teaspoon chipotle powder
½ teaspoon ground cumin
pinch of chilli flakes

01 Heat oil in a pan, add onion and cook gently until caramelised. Increase heat to medium–high, add remaining ingredients, stir, then simmer until mixture is reduced by half. Chill for up to 2 weeks.

Nutrition per serving:
42 cals / 2 g fat / 7 g carbs /
1 g fibre / 6 g net carbs /
1 g protein

Coconut butter

MAKES: 240 G (8½ OZ)
SERVING SIZE:
1 TABLESPOON
PREP / COOK TIME
15 minutes / 0 minutes

225 g (8 oz) shredded coconut
1 teaspoon sea salt

01 Combine ingredients in a high-powered blender or food processor and blend until smooth. Store in a cool, dry place for up to 2 weeks.

Nutrition per serving:
91 cals / 9 g fat / 1 g carbs /
0 g fibre / 1 g net carbs /
1 g protein

SMOKY
TOMATO
JAM

COCONUT
BUTTER

AVOCADO
OIL MAYO

Tahini herb dressing

MAKES: 240 ML (8 FL OZ)
SERVING SIZE: 45 ML (1½ FL OZ)
PREP / COOK TIME

15 minutes / 0 minutes

60 ml (¼ cup) extra virgin
  olive oil
1 tablespoon MCT oil
60 ml (¼ cup) tahini
3 tablespoons lemon juice
1 tablespoon grated
  lemon zest
2 teaspoons Dijon mustard
2 tablespoons each chopped
  dill, parsley and coriander
  (cilantro) leaves
1 teaspoon chopped thyme
salt and pepper

01 Place olive oil, MCT oil, tahini,
lemon juice, lemon zest and mustard
in a bowl and whisk together until
smooth, adding a little water as
necessary. Add herbs and mix until
combined. Season to taste. Store
in fridge for a week.

Nutrition per serving:
218 cals / 23 g fat / 3.5 g carbs /
1.3 g fibre / 2.2 g net carbs /
2.2 g protein

Blue cheese dressing

MAKES: 300 ML (10 FL OZ)
SERVING SIZE: 40 ML (1¼ FL OZ)
PREP / COOK TIME

15 minutes / 0 minutes

60 ml (¼ cup) buttermilk
60 ml (¼ cup) sour cream
2 tablespoons Avocado Oil
  Mayo (p. 74)
1 tablespoon avocado oil
1 teaspoon white wine vinegar
115 g (4 oz) blue cheese,
  crumbled
1 tablespoon finely chopped
  parsley
1 tablespoon finely chopped
  shallot
salt and pepper

01 Place buttermilk, sour cream,
mayo, oil, vinegar and blue cheese
in a bowl and whisk together until
combined well. Fold in remaining
ingredients. Season to taste. Store
in fridge for up to a week.

Nutrition per serving:
117 cals / 12 g fat / 2 g carbs /
0 g fibre / 2 g net carbs /
1 g protein

Avocado lime dressing

MAKES: 370 ML (12½ FL OZ)
SERVING SIZE: 40 ML (1¼ FL OZ)
PREP / COOK TIME

15 minutes / 0 minutes

60 ml (¼ cup) lime juice
180 ml (6 fl oz) avocado oil
2 tablespoons white wine
  vinegar
½ teaspoon very finely
  chopped garlic
3 tablespoons chopped
  coriander (cilantro) leaves
1 avocado, roughly chopped
1 small jalapeno (optional)
salt and pepper

01 Combine all ingredients in
a blender or food processor and
blend until combined. Season to
taste. Store in fridge for a week.

Nutrition per serving:
149 cals / 16 g fat / 3 g carbs /
1g fibre / 2 g net carbs /
0 g protein

TAHINI HERB
DRESSING

AVOCADO LIME
DRESSING

BLUE CHEESE
DRESSING

Harissa

MAKES: 220 G (8 OZ)
SERVING SIZE:
1 TABLESPOON
PREP / COOK TIME
15 minutes / 0 minutes

115 g (4 oz) dried ancho chilli,
  deseeded and soaked
1 teaspoon caraway seeds
1 teaspoon coriander seeds
1 teaspoon cumin seeds
3 garlic cloves, smashed
60 ml (¼ cup) extra virgin
  olive oil
2 tablespoons passata (pureed
  tomatoes)
1 teaspoon salt

01 Pat chilli dry with paper towel
and chop. Add chilli and spices
to a food processor and process
until finely ground. Add remaining
ingredients and process until well
blended. Place in a jar and store
in fridge for up to a month.

Nutrition per serving:
57 cals / 4 g fat / 4.4 g carbs /
1.7 g fibre/ 2.7 g net carbs /
1 g protein

Tzatziki

MAKES: 300 ML (10 FL OZ)
SERVING SIZE: 60 ML
(¼ CUP)
PREP / COOK TIME
15–20 minutes / 0 minutes

2 short cucumbers, grated
½ teaspoon salt, plus extra
  to serve
2 g (¹⁄₁₆ oz) dill, chopped
1 garlic clove
1 tablespoon MCT oil
juice of ½ lemon
240 ml (8 fl oz) full-fat Greek
  yoghurt

01 Place grated cucumbers in a
colander, sprinkle with salt and
toss together. Drain over a sink for
5 minutes, then squeeze out excess
moisture. Place cucumbers and
remaining ingredients in a bowl and
mix together until combined. Place
in a clean jar, seal and store in
fridge for up to a week.

Nutrition per serving:
84 cals / 8 g fat / 4.3 g carbs /
1 g fibre / 3.3 g net carbs /
2 g protein

Hollandaise

MAKES: 150 ML (5 FL OZ)
SERVING SIZE: 40 ML
(1¼ FL OZ)
PREP / COOK TIME
15 minutes / 0 minutes

130 g (4½ oz) ghee
1 large egg yolk
1 tablespoon lemon juice
salt and pepper

01 Heat ghee in a small pan until
hot. Place egg yolk and lemon juice
in a blender and blend. While motor
is still running, pour ghee in a slow,
steady stream until creamy. Season
to taste. Serve immediately.

Nutrition per serving:
196.2 cals / 22 g fat /
0.2 g carbs / 0 g fibre/
0.2 g net carbs / 0.5 g protein

TZATZIKI

HARISSA

HOLLANDAISE

Taco seasoning

MAKES: 8 G (⅓ OZ)
PREP / COOK TIME
5 minutes / 0 minutes

3 tablespoons chilli powder
2 tablespoons garlic powder
2 tablespoons onion powder
1 tablespoon ground cumin
1 tablespoon salt
2 teaspoons dried oregano
   (preferably Mexican)
1 teaspoon sweet paprika

01 Place ingredients in a small bowl and mix together until completely combined. Place in a jar and use when needed.

Nutrition:
171 cals / 1.8 g fat / 36.1 g carbs / 29.9 g fibre / 6.2 g net carbs / 7.5 g protein

Italian seasoning

MAKES: 30 G (1 OZ)
PREP / COOK TIME
5 minutes / 0 minutes

2 tablespoons dried oregano
2 tablespoons dried basil
1 tablespoon dried rosemary
1 tablespoon dried marjoram
1 tablespoon dried thyme
2 teaspoons garlic powder
1 teaspoon onion powder

01 Place ingredients in a small bowl and mix together until completely combined. Place in a jar and use when needed.

Nutrition:
80 cals / 1 g fat / 17.5 g carbs / 8.2 g fibre / 9.3 g net carbs / 3 g protein

Mediterranean seasoning

MAKES: 33 G (1 OZ)
PREP / COOK TIME
5 minutes / 0 minutes

3 tablespoons ground cumin
3 tablespoons ground
   coriander
1 tablespoon smoked paprika
1 teaspoon ground cinnamon

01 Place ingredients in a small bowl and mix together until completely combined. Place in a jar and use when needed.

Nutrition:
98 cals / 4 g fat / 10.1 g carbs / 3.3 g fibre / 6.8 g net carbs / 3.3 g protein

TACO SEASONING

ITALIAN SEASONING

MEDITERRANEAN SEASONING

Herb pesto

MAKES: 350 ML (12 FL OZ)
SERVINGS: 12
PREP / COOK TIME
15 minutes / 0 minutes

35 g (1¼ oz) brazil nuts,
  roughly chopped
1 garlic clove, smashed
50 g (1¾ oz) basil leaves,
  roughly chopped
60 g (2 oz) parsley, roughly
  chopped
10 g (⅓ oz) mint leaves,
  roughly chopped
115 g (4 oz) pecorino, grated
180 ml (6 fl oz) extra virgin
  olive oil
salt

01 Place brazil nuts and garlic in
a food processor and process until
ground. Add remaining ingredients,
except oil and salt, and pulse until
mixture is coarse. While motor is
running, pour oil in a slow, steady
stream until pesto is mostly smooth.
Season with salt. Store in fridge
for 5–7 days.

Nutrition per serving:
194 cals / 20 g fat / 2.3 g carbs /
0.4 g fibre / 1.9 g net carbs /
3.4 g protein

Sundried tomato pesto

MAKES: 350 ML (12 FL OZ)
SERVINGS: 12
15 minutes / 0 minutes

225 g (8 oz) sundried
  tomatoes in oil
110 g (4 oz) walnuts, toasted
3 garlic cloves
110 g (4 oz) parmesan, grated
120 ml (4 fl oz) extra virgin
  olive oil
salt

01 Place ingredients in a food
processor, except oil and salt, and
pulse until mixture is coarse. While
motor is running, pour oil in a slow,
steady stream until pesto is mostly
smooth. Season with salt.

Nutrition per serving:
238 cals / 23 g fat / 4 g carbs /
0.1 g fibre / 3.9 g net carbs /
4.3 g protein

Garlic aioli

MAKES: 120 ML (4 FL OZ)
SERVINGS: 6 (¾ FL OZ)
PREP / COOK TIME
15 minutes / 0 minutes

3 roasted garlic cloves (p. 72)
1 large egg yolk, at room
  temperature
½ teaspoon lemon juice
½ teaspoon salt
120 ml (4 fl oz) avocado oil
salt

01 Place ingredients, except oil and
salt, in a blender and blend until
creamy. While motor is running,
pour oil in a slow, steady stream
until creamy and thick. Season with
salt. Store in fridge for 2–3 days.

Nutrition per serving:
172 cals / 19 g fat / 7 g carbs /
0 g fibre / 7 g net carbs /
5 g protein

HERB PESTO

SUNDRIED TOMATO PESTO

GARLIC AIOLI

SEEDED KETO BREAD

....

Standard, flour-based loaves are off limits when eating keto, but this seed- and nut-based 'bread' is a high-fat, low-carb alternative.

MAKES: 1 LOAF / 15 SLICES
PREP / COOK TIME
10 minutes / 1 hour

70 g (2½ oz) pistachios
60 g (2 oz) hazelnuts
60 g (2 oz) linseeds (flax seeds)
50 g (1¾ oz) walnuts
50 g (⅓ cup) toasted sesame seeds
70 g (2½ oz) macadamia nuts
50 g (⅓ cup) pumpkin seeds
4 tablespoons psyllium seed husks
5 eggs
60 ml (¼ cup) coconut oil or ghee
½ teaspoon salt

01 Mix ingredients together in a large bowl, then pour into a greased 23 x 13 cm (9 x 5 in) loaf (bar) tin. Bake in oven (do not preheat oven) at 190°C (375°F) for 1 hour, or until firm. Remove from oven and leave to cool. Remove loaf from tin when completely cooled.

Nutrition per slice:
231 cals / 20 g fat / 8.1 g carbs / 5.4 g fibre / 2.7 g net carbs / 6.9 g protein

KETO 'OAT' MEAL BASE

Grains are off limits when eating a keto diet, but this porridge-like, low-carb replacement provides a versatile breakfast alternative.

SERVINGS: 10
PREP / COOK TIME
10 minutes / 5 minutes

115 g (4 oz) almond flour
50 g (1¾ oz) ground linseeds
  (flax seeds)
80 g (2¾ oz) chia seeds
80 g (2¾ oz) hemp seeds
40 g (1½ oz) collagen powder
110 g (4 oz) toasted pecan
  pieces
3 egg yolks, whisked
480 ml (16 fl oz) tinned
  coconut milk

01 Combine all dry ingredients together in a jar for easier use, then combine the beaten egg yolks and coconut milk in a separate jar. When ready to use, scoop 60 g (2 oz) of dry and 60 ml (¼ cup) of wet, plus 60 ml (¼ cup) water into a saucepan and cook over medium heat, stirring constantly, for 3–5 minutes. Add toppings as liked.

Note: Store the wet ingredients in fridge for 3–4 days.

Nutrition per serving:
357 cals / 30 g fat / 10.8 g carbs / 7.3 g fibre / 3.5 g net carbs / 13 g protein

KETO PANCAKE BASE

Just because grains are off limits, doesn't mean pancakes are. Ground macadamia nuts add healthy fat to this keto-friendly recipe that makes use of alternative flours.

SERVINGS: 3–4
PREP / COOK TIME
4 minutes / 10–15 minutes

75 g (2¾ oz) almond flour
40 g (1½ oz) coconut flour
3 tablespoons ground
   macadamia nuts
1 teaspoon baking powder
180 ml (6 fl oz) tinned coconut
   milk
3 large eggs
1 tablespoon MCT oil
2 teaspoons monkfruit
   sweetener

01 Combine dry ingredients in a small bowl and mix thoroughly. Whisk together wet ingredients in a medium bowl until combined, then add dry to wet ingredients and mix until combined. Heat coconut oil or butter in a frying pan over medium heat. Add 1 ladleful of batter into pan and flip when little bubbles rise to the top and bottom is brown, about 2–5 minutes. Remove and repeat to make 6–8 pancakes.

Nutrition per serving:
352.4 cals / 30 g fat / 12.4 g carbs / 5.8 g fibre / 6.6 g net carbs / 10.9 g protein

MORNING BEVERAGES

Adding fat to a morning cup of coffee, also known as bulletproof coffee, is a fat-friendly way to start the day. Some people even use it as a meal replacement, as the fat is very satiating. Turmeric-infused golden milk is another warm morning beverage.

Bulletproof coffee

SERVINGS: 1
PREP / COOK TIME
5 minutes / 0 minutes

240 ml (8 fl oz) hot coffee
1 tablespoon MCT or
  coconut oil
30 ml (1 fl oz) or more double
  (heavy) cream (optional)

01 Place ingredients in a blender and blend until frothy. Pour into a mug and serve immediately.

Nutrition per serving:
119 cals / 14 g fat / 1 g carbs /
1 g fibre / 0 g net carbs /
0 g protein

Golden milk

SERVINGS: 4
PREP / COOK TIME
5 minutes / 15 minutes

240 ml (8 fl oz) almond or
  coconut milk
1 cinnamon stick
½ teaspoon ground turmeric
  or 3 cm (1¼ in) knob fresh
  turmeric, thinly sliced
2 cm (¾ in) knob fresh ginger,
  thinly sliced
1 tablespoon MCT or
  coconut oil
¼ teaspoon coarsely
  ground pepper

01 Combine ingredients in a pan and whisk together. Add 240 ml (8 fl oz) water and simmer for 15 minutes. Strain and serve at once. Alternatively, store in fridge and slowly warm to serve.

Nutrition per serving:
54 cals / 5 g fat / 3.3 g carbs /
0.9 g fibre / 2.4 g net carbs /
1 g protein

GOLDEN MILK

BULLETPROOF
COFFEE

CAULIFLOWER PIZZA CRUST

Cauliflower pizza crust is a delicious keto-friendly alternative to standard, flour-based pizza dough.

MAKES: 8 SLICES
PREP / COOK TIME
10 minutes / 45 minutes

900 g (2 lb) Cauli-rice (p. 72)
3 eggs
1½ teaspoons Italian seasoning
  (p. 80)
50 g (½ cup) grated parmesan
55 g (⅓ cup) grated mozzarella
1 tablespoon MCT oil
1 tablespoon olive oil

01 Preheat oven to 200°C (400°F). Place cauli-rice in a nut bag or in a piece of muslin (cheesecloth) and squeeze dry to remove excess water. Place in a large bowl along with remaining ingredients and mix together. Spread mixture onto a lined baking tray into shape of pizza crust and bake for 30–35 minutes, until dry and golden. Flip and bake for another 10 minutes. Add toppings and bake for 5–10 minutes, until cheese is bubbly.

Nutrition per untopped slice:
113 cals / 9 g fat / 3.1 g carbs / 0.7 g fibre / 2.4 g net carbs / 6.8 g protein

KETO-FRIENDLY MARINARA

This tomato-based sauce contains no added sugar, unlike most store-bought options.

MAKES: 1.5 LITRES (6 CUPS)
PREP / COOK TIME
10 minutes / 45 minutes

5 tablespoons extra virgin
  olive oil
100 g (3½ oz) onion, chopped
6 garlic cloves, very finely
  chopped
2 anchovies in oil
790 g (1 lb 12 oz) tinned
  whole tomatoes, crushed
  by hand
2 teaspoons chopped parsley
1 teaspoon chopped oregano
salt and pepper

01 Heat olive oil in a pan over medium–high heat, add onion and cook until translucent. Reduce heat to medium, add garlic and anchovies and stir for 1–2 minutes. Add tomatoes and herbs and bring to a simmer. Simmer for 45 minutes. Season. Cool to room temperature. This can be made 3–5 days in advance and stored in fridge.

Nutrition:
1002 cals / 68 g fat / 81.9 g carbs / 15.8 g fibre / 66.1 g net carbs / 16.6 g protein

28 DAYS OF MEALS

In order to make your transition to eating keto as simple and manageable (and delicious!) as possible, the recipes in this section are organised by day, with three meals (breakfast, lunch and dinner) that fit the general parameters of a low-carb, high-fat, medium-protein diet to help jumpstart ketosis and its many benefits. The days are organised by weeks, each one with an associated shopping list and tips for what can be prepped ahead of time on the weekend, so you are not spending hours trying to make a weekday meal.

WEEK 1
WEEKLY SHOPPING LIST

FRUIT
- [ ] raspberries
- [ ] blackberries
- [ ] lemon – 3
- [ ] avocado – 3
- [ ] physalis – 2

VEGETABLES
- [ ] rocket (arugula) – 80 g (2¾ oz)
- [ ] frisee (curly endive) – 1 head
- [ ] mixed leaves – 75 g (2¾ oz)
- [ ] butter (bibb) lettuce – 1 head
- [ ] cabbage – ¼ head
- [ ] kale – 1 small bunch
- [ ] heirloom tomatoes – 2 medium
- [ ] cherry tomatoes – 300 g (10½ oz)
- [ ] cucumbers – 2
- [ ] beetroot (beets) – 3 large
- [ ] brown onion – 3 large
- [ ] red onion – 1 small
- [ ] spring onions (scallions) –1 small bunch
- [ ] shallot – 4
- [ ] garlic – 2 bulbs
- [ ] ginger – 1 small piece
- [ ] carrot –1 large
- [ ] fennel bulb – 1
- [ ] broccoli – 1 small head
- [ ] cauliflower –1.5 kg (3 lb 5 oz)
- [ ] eggplants (aubergines) – 2 large, 1 medium
- [ ] spaghetti squash – 1
- [ ] Calabrian chilli or chilli flakes
- [ ] parsley, coriander (cilantro), mint, thyme, oregano, chives, dill, basil – 1 bunch each

PROTEINS
- [ ] whole chicken – 2.6 kg (5¾ lb)
- [ ] chicken thigh fillets (skinless) – 180 g (6½ oz)
- [ ] rock cod fillet – 175 g (6 oz)
- [ ] bacon strips – 100 g (3½ oz)
- [ ] guanciale – 115 g (4 oz)
- [ ] prosciutto – 12 slices
- [ ] smoked salmon – 125 g (4½ oz)

DAIRY/EGGS
- [ ] double (heavy) cream – 1 small pot
- [ ] almond milk
- [ ] full fat Greek yoghurt
- [ ] buttermilk
- [ ] sour cream
- [ ] full-fat kefir
- [ ] labneh
- [ ] unsalted butter
- [ ] stilton/blue cheese – 200 g (7 oz)
- [ ] bocconcini mozzarella – 200 g (7 oz)
- [ ] mozzarella, grated – 340 g (12 oz)
- [ ] pecorino – 215 g (7½ oz)
- [ ] parmesan, grated – 100 g (3½ oz)
- [ ] ricotta – 475 g (1 lb 1 oz)
- [ ] goat's cheese – 75 g (2¾ oz)
- [ ] large eggs – 12

FROZEN
- [ ] frozen edamame – 1 packet

CHECK TO SEE IF IN PANTRY
- [ ] extra virgin olive oil
- [ ] avocado oil
- [ ] ghee
- [ ] MCT oil
- [ ] coconut oil
- [ ] toasted sesame oil
- [ ] balsamic vinegar
- [ ] apple cider vinegar
- [ ] white wine vinegar
- [ ] tin whole tomatoes – 800 g (1 lb 12 oz)
- [ ] passata (pureed tomatoes)
- [ ] anchovy fillets in oil
- [ ] low-carb chicken stock cubes
- [ ] tamari
- [ ] brazil nuts
- [ ] macadamia nuts
- [ ] pine nuts
- [ ] walnuts
- [ ] chia seeds
- [ ] hemp seeds
- [ ] linseeds (flax seeds)
- [ ] toasted sesame seeds
- [ ] almond flour
- [ ] vanilla extract
- [ ] ground cinnamon
- [ ] ground cumin
- [ ] curry powder
- [ ] ground turmeric
- [ ] smoked paprika
- [ ] monkfruit sweetener
- [ ] cacao powder
- [ ] cacao nibs
- [ ] protein powder
- [ ] Dijon mustard
- [ ] tahini
- [ ] full-fat coconut milk – 220 ml (7½ fl oz)

WEEK 1 PREP

Check to see if you have any of these basics already made and if not, add ingredients to your shopping list.

BASICS
(these are items that you should have pre-prepped as they will last a while)

- [ ] Keto 'Oat'meal Base, dry and wet (p. 86)
- [ ] Coconut Flax Granola (p. 172)
- [ ] Mediterranean Seasoning (p. 80)
- [ ] Seeded Keto Bread (p. 84)

PREP

- [ ] Cauliflower for Cauli-rice (p. 72)
- [ ] Cauliflower Pizza Crust (p. 92)
- [ ] Cinnamon Porridge, dry ingredients (p. 102)
- [ ] Boil egg(s) for Cobb Salad (p. 110)

MAKE

- [ ] Chia Pudding (p. 104)
- [ ] Avocado Oil Mayo (p. 74)
- [ ] Blue Cheese Dressing (p. 76)
- [ ] Keto-friendly Marinara (p. 94) for Eggplant Lasagne (p. 104)

- [ ] Herb Pesto (p. 82) for Roasted Spaghetti Squash with Herb Pesto (p. 112)
- [ ] Beetroot Dip (p. 182) for Mediterranean 'Meat'Balls (p. 106)
- [ ] Tzatziki (p. 78) for Chicken & Eggplant Bowl (p. 112)

ROAST

- [ ] Spaghetti squash for Roasted Spaghetti Squash with Herb Pesto (p. 112)
- [ ] Beetroot (beets) for Beetroot Dip (p. 182)
- [ ] Cauliflower Pizza Crust (p. 92)

WEEK 1 TIMETABLE

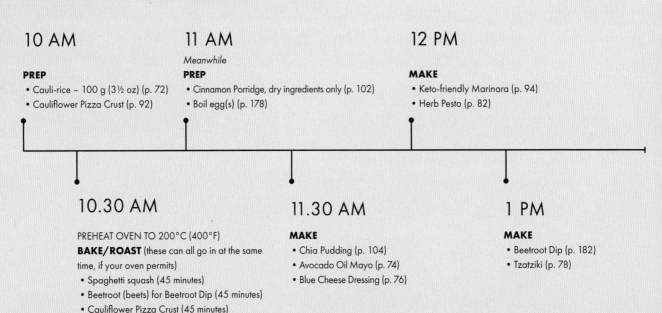

10 AM

PREP
- Cauli-rice – 100 g (3½ oz) (p. 72)
- Cauliflower Pizza Crust (p. 92)

11 AM

Meanwhile

PREP
- Cinnamon Porridge, dry ingredients only (p. 102)
- Boil egg(s) (p. 178)

12 PM

MAKE
- Keto-friendly Marinara (p. 94)
- Herb Pesto (p. 82)

10.30 AM

PREHEAT OVEN TO 200°C (400°F)
BAKE/ROAST (these can all go in at the same time, if your oven permits)
- Spaghetti squash (45 minutes)
- Beetroot (beets) for Beetroot Dip (45 minutes)
- Cauliflower Pizza Crust (45 minutes)

11.30 AM

MAKE
- Chia Pudding (p. 104)
- Avocado Oil Mayo (p. 74)
- Blue Cheese Dressing (p. 76)

1 PM

MAKE
- Beetroot Dip (p. 182)
- Tzatziki (p. 78)

ROAST SPAGHETTI SQUASH

1. Roast squash for 45 minutes

2. Use fork to gently scrape flesh into strands

3. Continue until all flesh is in strands

4. Transfer to bowl

DAY

01

MONDAY

Today's dinner recipe makes enough roast chicken for you to use in other recipes throughout the week.

BREAKFAST

Cinnamon porridge

SERVINGS: 1
PREP / COOK TIME
5 minutes / 10 minutes

4 tablespoons almond flour
2 tablespoons ground linseeds (flax seeds)
160 ml (5½ fl oz) coconut milk
1 tablespoon coconut oil
pinch of salt
1 teaspoon ground cinnamon, plus extra
   for topping
6 raspberries

01 Combine flour, linseeds, milk, oil, salt, cinnamon and 100 ml (3½ fl oz) water in a pan over medium heat and stir until mixture begins to thicken. Transfer to a bowl and top with raspberries and extra cinnamon. Serve.

Nutrition per serving:
383 cals / 34 g fat / 14.5 g carbs /
9.3 g fibre / 5.2 g net carbs / 9 g protein

LUNCH

Avocado & prosciutto salad with blue cheese

SERVINGS: 1
PREP / COOK TIME
5 minutes / 0 minutes

75 g (2¾ oz) mixed leaves
1 avocado, chopped
6 prosciutto slices
60 ml (¼ cup) Blue Cheese Dressing
   (p. 76)
salt and pepper

01 Place mixed leaves in a bowl and top with avocado and prosciutto. Top with dressing and season to taste.

Nutrition per serving:
578 cals / 47 g fat / 20.9 g carbs /
11.7 g fibre / 9.2 g net carbs / 23 g protein
(without blue cheese dressing)

DINNER

Roast chicken with vegetables

SERVINGS: 4
PREP / COOK TIME
5 minutes / 45–55 minutes

1 whole chicken, (about 2.6 kg/5¾ lb)
salt and pepper
1 large onion, chopped
1 large carrot, chopped
1 fennel bulb, sliced into 3 cm (1¼ in)
   slices
3 parsley sprigs, chopped
2 thyme sprigs, chopped
6 garlic cloves, smashed
1 lemon, sliced
70 g (2½ oz) ghee

01 Preheat oven to 220°C (430°F). Season chicken generously. Place all ingredients, except chicken and ghee, into a roasting tin and toss together. Rub ghee over chicken and place on top of vegetables. Roast for 45–55 minutes, until completely cooked through, rotating halfway. Serve sliced with vegetables. Shred left-over chicken for packed lunches.

Nutrition per serving:
759 cals / 51 g fat / 14 g carbs / 3.6 g fibre /
10.4 g net carbs / 60 g protein

**ROAST CHICKEN
WITH VEGETABLES**

**CINNAMON
PORRIDGE**

**AVOCADO & PROSCIUTTO
SALAD WITH BLUE CHEESE**

DAY

02

TUESDAY

Today's berry chia seed pudding can be prepped ahead of time, for a quick and easy breakfast on the go.

BREAKFAST

Berry chia seed pudding

SERVINGS: 1
PREP / CHILL TIME
5 minutes / 1 hour–overnight

2 tablespoons chia seeds
180 ml (6 fl oz) almond milk
1 teaspoon vanilla extract
1½ teaspoons monkfruit sweetener
pinch of salt
3 raspberries
2 blackberries, halved

01 Place chia seeds, milk, vanilla, sweetener and salt in a jar and stir together. Chill in fridge for at least 1 hour, or overnight. When ready to serve, top with berries.

Nutrition per serving:
149 cals / 8 g fat / 12.8 g carbs /
8.1 g fibre / 4.7 g net carbs / 4.7 g protein

LUNCH

Curry chicken with cauli-rice

SERVINGS: 1
PREP / COOK TIME
15 minutes / 10 minutes

2 shallots, thinly sliced
75 g (2¾ oz) shredded chicken from Roast
  Chicken with Vegetables (p. 102)
25 g (1 oz) broccoli, chopped
2 tablespoons chopped coriander (cilantro)
  leaves, plus extra to garnish
1 tablespoon curry powder
4 tablespoons Avocado Oil Mayo (p. 74)
salt and pepper
2 tablespoons ghee
100 g (3½ oz) Cauli-rice (p. 72)

01 Mix shallots, chicken, broccoli, coriander, curry powder and mayo together in a bowl until thoroughly combined. Season with salt and set aside. Heat ghee in a frying pan until melted. Add cauli-rice and cook for 3–4 minutes. Season to taste. Transfer to a plate and top with curry chicken. Top with extra coriander.

Nutrition per serving:
834 cals / 57 g fat / 51 g carbs /
14 g fibre / 37 g net carbs / 30 g protein

DINNER

Eggplant lasagne

SERVINGS: 12
PREP / COOK TIME
20 minutes / 1 hour

2 eggplants (aubergines), cut into
  4 cm (1½ in) slices
salt and pepper
475 g (1 lb 1 oz) ricotta
1 egg
170 g (6 oz) mozzarella, grated
1 x quantity Keto-friendly Marinara (p. 94)
50 g (½ cup) grated parmesan

01 Salt eggplant with 1 teaspoon salt on both sides and leave for 10 minutes. Pat dry. In a pan, lightly brown both sides of eggplant. Set aside.

02 Preheat oven to 190°C (375°F). Combine ricotta and egg. Season. Grease a 23 x 30 cm (9 x 12 in) baking dish. Spread half the sauce over base and cover with half the eggplant. Spread with half the ricotta mix, then a layer of mozzarella and repeat, finishing with parmesan. Cover and bake for 40 minutes. Uncover and bake for 10 minutes. Serve. Freeze any remaining for another meal.

Nutrition per serving:
258 cals / 14 g fat / 15.3 g carbs /
5.1 g fibre / 10.2 g net carbs / 17 g protein

BERRY CHIA
SEED PUDDING

CURRY CHICKEN
WITH CAULI-RICE

EGGPLANT
LASAGNE

WEDNESDAY

Physalis are the lowest carb-per-serving berry, which makes them a great way to sweeten your breakfast. They are also a nutrient-packed food.

....

BREAKFAST

'Oat'meal with physalis & nuts

SERVINGS: 1
PREP / COOK TIME
5 minutes / 5 minutes

1 × serving Keto 'Oat'meal Base (p. 86)
½ teaspoon ground turmeric
½ teaspoon ground cinnamon
2 tablespoons double (heavy) cream
1 tablespoon MCT oil
1 teaspoon monkfruit sweetener
2 tablespoons macadamia nuts, chopped
15 g (½ oz) physalis

01 Place 'oat'meal base and remaining ingredients, except nuts and physalis, in a pan over medium heat and warm, stirring constantly, for 3–5 minutes. Add nuts and physalis to serve.

Nutrition per serving:
368 cals / 35 g fat / 14.1 g carbs / 5.3 g fibre / 8.8 g net carbs / 3 g protein

LUNCH

Prosciutto & goat's cheese salad

SERVINGS: 1
PREP / COOK TIME
5 minutes / 0 minutes

40 g (1½ oz) rocket (arugula)
30 g (1 oz) frisee (curly endive), torn into bite-sized pieces
6 prosciutto slices
30 g (1 oz) goat's cheese, crumbled
2 tablespoons walnuts, toasted
3 tablespoons extra virgin olive oil
2 teaspoons apple cider vinegar
salt and pepper

01 Arrange rocket and frisee on a plate or in a container. Top with remaining ingredients and drizzle with oil and vinegar. Season.

Nutrition per serving:
633 cals / 60 g fat / 4.7 g carbs / 2 g fibre / 2.7 g net carbs / 21.4 g protein

DINNER

Mediterranean 'meat'balls

SERVINGS: 4
PREP / COOK TIME
5 minutes / 20–25 minutes

30 g (1 oz) parsley, chopped
3 tablespoons chopped mint leaves
200 g (7 oz) onion, grated
3 tablespoons pine nuts, roughly chopped
2½ teaspoons Mediterranean Seasoning (p. 80)
1 teaspoon sea salt
1 teaspoon ground black pepper
60 g (2 oz) Beetroot Dip (p. 182)
6 tablespoons labneh

01 Preheat oven to 230°C (445°F). Combine parsley, mint, onion, pine nuts, seasoning, salt and pepper and half the beetroot dip in a bowl. Using a heaped tablespoon, form mixture into 12–16 'meat'balls. Place 'meat'balls on a lined baking tray and bake for 20–25 minutes, rotating halfway through. Serve with remaining beetroot dip and labneh. Freeze remaining 'meat'balls for another day.

Nutrition per serving:
507 cals / 34 g fat / 12.2 g carbs / 2.8 g fibre / 9.4 g net carbs / 37 g protein

'OAT'MEAL WITH
PHYSALIS & NUTS

PROSCIUTTO &
GOAT'S CHEESE
SALAD

MEDITERRANEAN
'MEAT'BALLS

DAY

04

THURSDAY

Save time by using left-over roast chicken from day 1 to make today's caprese salad lunch.

BREAKFAST

Cacao smoothie bowl

SERVINGS: 1
PREP / COOK TIME
5 minutes / 0 minutes

60 ml (¼ cup) full-fat coconut milk
30 g (1 oz) zero-carb protein powder
½ avocado
1 tablespoon cacao powder
1 tablespoon MCT oil
5 g (¼ oz) cacao nibs
1 tablespoon hemp seeds

01 Place coconut milk, protein powder and avocado in a blender, together with 250 g (9 oz) ice. Slowly add MCT oil while blending. Pour into a bowl and top with cacao nibs and hemp seeds. Serve immediately.

Nutrition per serving:
537 cals / 44 g fat / 13 g carbs / 7.5 g fibre /
5.5 g net carbs / 31.9 g protein

LUNCH

Chicken caprese salad with rocket

SERVINGS: 1
PREP / COOK TIME
5 minutes / 0 minutes

2 tablespoons balsamic vinegar
3 tablespoons extra virgin olive oil
salt and pepper
40 g (1½ oz) rocket (arugula)
75 g (2¾ oz) shredded chicken from Roast Chicken with Vegetables (p. 102)
5 cherry tomatoes, halved
3 bocconcini mozzarella balls, quartered
½ avocado, thinly sliced
8 g (¼ oz) basil leaves

01 Mix vinegar and oil together until emulsified, then season with salt and pepper. Place rocket in a bowl and top with remaining ingredients. Drizzle with balsamic oil mixture and season with salt and pepper.

Nutrition per serving:
867 cals / 72 g fat / 14.5 g carbs /
5.9 g fibre / 8.6 g net carbs / 42 g protein

DINNER

Rock cod in spicy tomato broth

SERVINGS: 1
PREP / COOK TIME
10 minutes / 20–30 minutes

2 tablespoons extra virgin olive oil
½ shallot, thinly sliced
1 garlic clove, thinly sliced
1 Calabrian chilli, chopped, or chilli flakes
1 tablespoon passata (pureed tomatoes)
100 g (3½ oz) cherry tomatoes
60 ml (¼ cup) stock made from low-carb stock cube dissolved in 240 ml (8 fl oz) water
175 g (6 oz) rock cod (Pacific rockfish) fillet
1½ tablespoons unsalted butter
salt and pepper
1 tablespoon chopped parsley, to garnish

01 Heat oil in a pan, add shallot and cook until translucent. Stir in garlic, chilli, passata and tomatoes. Cook until tomatoes burst. Stir in stock. Add cod and butter and simmer, covered, for 10–15 minutes, until cod is cooked through. Season. Garnish with parsley.

Nutrition per serving:
575 cals / 40 g fat / 11.7 g carbs /
2.8 g fibre / 8.9 g net carbs / 41 g protein

CACAO SMOOTHIE BOWL

CHICKEN CAPRESE SALAD
WITH ROCKET

ROCK COD IN SPICY
TOMATO BROTH

FRIDAY

Top your already made cauliflower crust with kale, cheese and guanciale for today's delicious dinner, and you won't even miss carb-heavy pizza.

BREAKFAST

Kefir bowl with granola

SERVINGS: 1
PREP / COOK TIME
5 minutes / 0 minutes

120 ml (4 fl oz) full-fat kefir
1 tablespoon MCT oil
24 g (1 oz) protein powder
30 g (1 oz) Coconut Flax Granola
  (p. 172)

01 Mix kefir, MCT oil and protein powder together in a bowl until thoroughly combined. Top with granola.

Nutrition per serving:
438 cals / 34.5 g fat / 13.4 g carbs /
3 g fibre / 10.4 g net carbs / 25 g protein

LUNCH

Cobb salad

SERVINGS: 1
PREP / COOK TIME
10 minutes / 0 minutes

85 g (3 oz) butter lettuce
170 g (6 oz) cherry tomatoes, halved
75 g (2¾ oz) shredded chicken from Roast
  Chicken with Vegetables (p. 102)
¼ red onion, sliced
100 g (3½ oz) bacon strips, cooked
85 g (3 oz) stilton, crumbled
1 large medium-boiled egg, halved
60 ml (¼ cup) Blue Cheese Dressing
  (p. 76)
salt and pepper

01 Place lettuce in bowl or container and top with remaining ingredients. Drizzle with dressing. Season and serve.

Nutrition per serving:
1023 cals / 80 g fat / 17.5 g carbs /
10.4 g fibre / 7.1 g net carbs / 61.5 g protein

DINNER

Pizza with guanciale & kale

SERVINGS: 4
PREP / COOK TIME
10 minutes / 10–15 minutes

30 g (1 oz) kale, stalks removed
  and leaves roughly chopped
juice of ½ lemon
60 ml (¼ cup) extra virgin olive oil
salt and pepper
1 Cauliflower Pizza Crust (p. 92)
115 g (4 oz) mozzarella, grated
50 g (1¾ oz) pecorino, grated, plus extra
  for top
115 g (4 oz) guanciale, very thinly sliced
1–2 tablespoons chopped Calabrian chilli
  or chilli flakes
2 garlic cloves, thinly sliced

01 Preheat oven to 200°C (400°F). Massage kale, lemon juice and 2 tablespoons oil together. Season. Top crust with half the cheeses, the guanciale, chilli, garlic, remaining oil and kale, then top with rest of cheese. Bake for 10–15 minutes, until cheese is bubbly. Cut into eight slices and serve. Store any remaining slices in fridge for another day.

Nutrition per serving:
328.2 cals / 29.1 g fat / 5.4 g carbs /
0.9 g fibre / 4.5 g net carbs / 13.6 g protein

KEFIR BOWL
WITH GRANOLA

PIZZA WITH
GUANCIALE & KALE

COBB SALAD

DAY

06

SATURDAY

Savoury breakfasts are more keto-friendly than sweet ones, but often more labour-intensive, so great for weekend eating, when you have more time.

BREAKFAST

Eggs in avocado with goat's cheese

SERVINGS: 1
PREP / COOK TIME
10 minutes / 15–20 minutes

1 avocado, sliced in half and stoned
2 large eggs
2 tablespoons crumbled goat's cheese
½ teaspoon smoked paprika
1 tablespoon finely diced red onion
2 tablespoons chopped coriander (cilantro) leaves
salt and pepper

01 Preheat oven to 220°C (430°F). Place avocado halves on a baking tray. Break an egg into each avocado half. Sprinkle with goat's cheese and paprika and bake for 15–20 minutes, until yolk consistency is to your liking. Top with onion and coriander and season with salt and pepper.

Nutrition per serving:
687 cals / 56 g fat / 14.1 g carbs / 9.5 g fibre / 4.6 g net carbs / 36 g protein

LUNCH

Chicken & eggplant bowl

SERVINGS: 1
PREP / COOK TIME
15 minutes / 20–30 minutes

85 g (3 oz) eggplant (aubergine), chopped
salt and pepper
3 tablespoons extra virgin olive oil
2 tablespoons lemon juice
3½ teaspoons Mediterranean Seasoning (p. 80)
1 garlic clove, very finely chopped
180 g (6½ oz) skinless chicken thigh fillets
35 g (1¼ oz) shredded cabbage
¼ red onion, thinly sliced
2 tablespoons chopped parsley leaves
2 tablespoons coriander (cilantro) leaves
30 ml (1 fl oz) Tzatziki (p. 78), to serve

01 Preheat oven to 190°C (375°F). Sprinkle eggplant with ½ teaspoon salt. Combine 2 tablespoons oil, lemon, seasoning and garlic, then add chicken. Toss eggplant with rest of oil. Bake chicken and eggplant for 25 minutes or until cooked. Cut chicken into slices. Put everything in a bowl. Season and serve with tzatziki.

Nutrition per serving:
665 cals / 51 g fat / 13 g carbs / 5.8 g fibre / 26 g net carbs / 38 g protein

DINNER

Roasted spaghetti squash with herb pesto

SERVINGS: 1
PREP / COOK TIME
10 minutes / 45 minutes

2 tablespoons extra virgin olive oil
75 g (2¾ oz) spaghetti squash, roasted and shredded
40 g (1½ oz) Herb Pesto (p. 82)
2 tablespoons grated pecorino
salt and pepper

01 Mix oil, spaghetti squash and pesto in a bowl until squash is coated. Top with cheese and season with salt and pepper. Serve.

Nutrition per serving:
506 cals / 50 g fat / 8.9 g carbs / 1.6 g fibre / 7.3 g net carbs / 7.5 g protein

**EGGS IN AVOCADO
WITH GOAT'S CHEESE**

**CHICKEN &
EGGPLANT
BOWL**

**ROASTED SPAGHETTI
SQUASH WITH HERB PESTO**

DAY
07

SUNDAY

If you have any left-over vegetables from earlier in the week, feel free
to add them to today's dinner, as long as they fit within your carb parameters.

BREAKFAST

Eggs florentine

SERVINGS: 1
PREP / COOK TIME
5 minutes / 10 minutes

1 slice Seeded Keto Bread (p. 84)
2 slices (125 g/4½ oz) smoked salmon
2 eggs, poached
1 serving Hollandaise (p. 78)
1 tablespoon chopped chives
salt and pepper

01 Place bread on a plate and top with remaining
ingredients. Season with salt and pepper.

Nutrition per serving:
730 cals / 59 g fat / 9.7 g carbs /
5.6 g fibre / 4.1 g net carbs / 42 g protein

LUNCH

Summer heirloom tomato salad with blue cheese dressing

SERVINGS: 1
PREP / COOK TIME
5 minutes / 0 minutes

2 medium heirloom tomatoes, sliced
2 tablespoons chives, chopped
2 tablespoons extra virgin olive oil
salt and pepper
60 ml (¼ cup) Blue Cheese Dressing
  (p. 76)
1 slice Seeded Keto Bread (p. 84)

01 Arrange tomatoes on a plate, top with chives
and drizzle with oil. Season with salt and pepper.
Serve with dressing and bread.

Nutrition per serving:
730 cals / 69 g fat / 19.4 g carbs /
8.5 g fibre / 10.9 g net carbs / 15 g protein

DINNER

Fried cauli-rice

SERVINGS: 1
PREP / COOK TIME
15 minutes / 10 minutes

1 tablespoon extra virgin olive oil
½ teaspoon grated ginger
30 g (1 oz) frozen edamame
1 garlic clove, very finely chopped
340 g (12 oz) Cauli-rice (p. 72)
1 egg, whisked
1½ tablespoons tamari
2 spring onions (scallions), thinly sliced
1 teaspoon toasted sesame oil
½ teaspoon toasted sesame seeds

01 Heat oil in a non-stick saucepan or wok over
medium heat, add ginger and edamame and
cook for 2–3 minutes. Add garlic and cauli-rice
and cook for another 2–3 minutes. Add egg,
tamari, half the spring onion and the sesame oil
and cook until egg is cooked through. Top with
remaining spring onion and sesame seeds.

Nutrition per serving:
243 cals / 15 g fat / 20.2 g carbs /
10 g fibre / 10.2 g net carbs / 11 g protein

EGGS FLORENTINE

**SUMMER HEIRLOOM TOMATO SALAD
WITH BLUE CHEESE DRESSING**

FRIED CAULI-RICE

WEEK 2
WEEKLY SHOPPING LIST

FRUIT

- [ ] raspberries
- [ ] blackberries
- [ ] strawberry
- [ ] lemon – 2
- [ ] lime – 4
- [ ] avocado –2

VEGETABLES

- [ ] cos (romaine) lettuce – 1 head
- [ ] little gem lettuce – 1 head
- [ ] butter (bibb) lettuce – 1 head
- [ ] iceberg lettuce – ½
- [ ] red cabbage – 1 small head
- [ ] kale – 1 bunch
- [ ] spring greens – 1 bunch
- [ ] cherry tomatoes – 135 g (5 oz)
- [ ] brown onion – 2 small
- [ ] red onion – 1 small
- [ ] shallot – 1
- [ ] spring onions (scallions) – 1 bunch
- [ ] garlic – 1 bulb
- [ ] ginger – 1 small piece
- [ ] cauliflower – 1 small head
- [ ] broccoli – 1 small head
- [ ] short cucumbers – 4
- [ ] zucchini (courgette) – 1
- [ ] asparagus - 1 bunch
- [ ] green beans – 85 g (3 oz)
- [ ] rainbow carrots – 1 bunch
- [ ] radishes – 1 bunch
- [ ] mixed mushrooms – 60 g (2 oz)
- [ ] eggplant (aubergine) – 1 large
- [ ] red bell pepper (capsicum) – 1
- [ ] porcini mushrooms – 80 g (2¾ oz)
- [ ] jalapenos – 2 small
- [ ] parsley, coriander (cilantro), dill and thyme – 1 bunch each

PROTEINS

- [ ] chicken thighs fillets (skinless) – 170 g (6 oz)
- [ ] beef chuck (braising) steak – 900 g (2 lb)
- [ ] oyster blade (flat iron) steak – 285 g (10 oz)
- [ ] rock cod – 2 x 170 g (6 oz) fillets
- [ ] mackerel fillet – 170 g (6 oz)
- [ ] prawns (shrimp) – 280 g (10 oz)

DAIRY/EGGS

- [ ] almond milk
- [ ] full-fat Greek yoghurt
- [ ] buttermilk
- [ ] sour cream
- [ ] kefir
- [ ] burrata
- [ ] cheddar – 35 g (1¼ oz)
- [ ] pecorino – 25 g (1 oz)
- [ ] parmesan – 50 g (1¾ oz)
- [ ] feta – 90 g (3 oz)
- [ ] blue cheese – 115 g (4 oz)
- [ ] eggs – 12
- [ ] unsalted butter

MISC

- [ ] Kalamata olives
- [ ] sake
- [ ] semi-dried tomatoes – 50 g (1¾ oz)

CHECK TO SEE IF IN PANTRY

- [ ] ghee
- [ ] MCT oil
- [ ] coconut oil
- [ ] extra virgin olive oil
- [ ] avocado oil
- [ ] toasted sesame oil
- [ ] red wine vinegar
- [ ] apple cider vinegar
- [ ] white wine vinegar
- [ ] tin chopped tomatoes – 400 g (14 oz)
- [ ] tinned tuna in oil – 125 g (4½ oz)
- [ ] chicken stock cubes
- [ ] coconut aminos or tamari
- [ ] fish sauce
- [ ] almond butter
- [ ] flaked almonds
- [ ] roasted pumpkin seeds
- [ ] almond flour
- [ ] coconut flour
- [ ] ground macadamias – 40 g (1½ oz)
- [ ] monkfruit sweetener
- [ ] shredded coconut
- [ ] ground golden linseeds (flax seeds)
- [ ] poppy seeds
- [ ] toasted sesame seeds
- [ ] Dijon mustard
- [ ] chia seeds
- [ ] full-fat coconut milk – 560 ml (2¼ cups)
- [ ] ground cinnamon
- [ ] ground cumin
- [ ] curry powder
- [ ] ground turmeric
- [ ] dried oregano
- [ ] chilli flakes
- [ ] chipotle chilli powder
- [ ] chipotle chilli in adobo
- [ ] pepperoncini peppers – 30 g (1 oz)
- [ ] capers
- [ ] matcha (green tea) powder

WEEK 2 PREP

....

Check to see if you have any of these basics already made and if not, add ingredients to your shopping list.

BASICS

(these are items that you should have pre-prepped as they will last a while)

- [ ] Smoky Tomato Jam (p. 74)
- [ ] Taco Seasoning (p. 80)
- [ ] Keto 'Oat'meal Base, dry and wet (p. 86)
- [ ] Keto Pancake Base mix (p. 88)
- [ ] Coconut Flax Granola (p. 172)

PREP

- [ ] Zoodles (p. 68)
- [ ] Cauliflower for Cauli-rice (p. 72)
- [ ] Hard-boil egg and blanch green beans for Niçoise Salad (p. 130)
- [ ] Grind macadamias for Coconut Prawns & Curried Vegetables (p. 124)
- [ ] Greek Salad (p. 122)
- [ ] Dark, Leafy Greens salad (p. 124)

MAKE

- [ ] Avocado Lime Dressing (p. 76)
- [ ] Avocado Oil Mayo (p. 74)
- [ ] Blue Cheese Dressing (p. 76)
- [ ] Garlic Aioli (p. 82)
- [ ] Matcha Kefir-chia Pudding (p. 128)

ROAST

- [ ] Garlic bulb for Garlic Aioli (p. 82)
- [ ] Vegetables for Eggplant Porcini Burgers (p. 122)

WEEK 2 TIMETABLE

10 AM

PREHEAT OVEN TO 200°C (400°C)
PREP
- Zoodles – 185 g (6 oz) (p. 68)
- Cauli-rice – 275 g (9½ oz) (p. 72)

11 AM

Meanwhile
MAKE
- Avocado Lime Dressing (p. 76)
- Avocado Oil Mayo (p. 74)
- Blue Cheese Dressing (p. 76)

1 PM

MAKE
- Garlic Aioli (p. 82)
- Eggplant Porcini Burgers (p. 122)
- Matcha Kefir-chia Pudding (p. 128)

10.30 AM

BAKE/ROAST (these can all go in at the same time, if your oven permits)
- Roast garlic bulb (45 minutes)
- Roast eggplant (aubergine) and bell peppers (capsicums) (30 minutes)

12 PM

PREP
- Hard-boil egg (p. 178) and blanch green beans (p. 130)
- Ground macadamias (p. 72)
- Greek Salad (p. 122)
- Dark, Leafy Greens salad (p. 124)

MAKE SPRING GREEN WRAPS

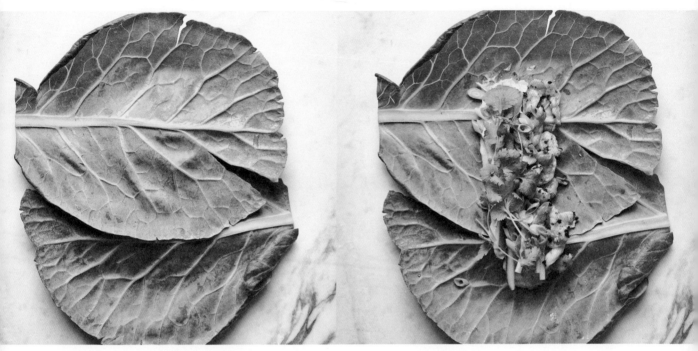

1. Place 2 spring green leaves on surface, making a large 20 x 12.5 cm (8 x 5 in) piece

2. Add filling down middle of wrap

3. Tightly roll up wrap

4. Serve

DAY

08

MONDAY

Today's smoky chilli dinner makes more than one serving. Freeze the leftovers for use on another day, when you don't have time to prep a meal from scratch.

....

BREAKFAST
Blackberry porridge

SERVINGS: 1
PREP / COOK TIME
5 minutes / 10 minutes

3 tablespoons almond flour
1 tablespoon ground golden linseeds (flax seeds)
120 ml (4 fl oz) full-fat coconut milk
1 tablespoon coconut oil
pinch of salt
70 g (2½ oz) blackberries

01 Combine flour, linseeds, milk, 100 ml (3½ fl oz) water, oil and salt in a saucepan over medium heat and stir until mixture begins to thicken. Transfer to a bowl and top with blackberries. Serve.

Nutrition per serving:
503 cals / 45 g fat / 18 g carbs / 10.1 g fibre / 7.9 g net carbs / 9.4 g protein

LUNCH
Cod à la meunière

SERVINGS: 1
PREP / COOK TIME
15 minutes / 30 minutes

3 teaspoons extra virgin olive oil
90 g (3 oz) broccoli, chopped
1 teaspoon chilli flakes
salt and pepper
2 tablespoons almond flour
1 tablespoon coconut flour
2 cod fillets (175 g / 6 oz each)
3 tablespoons ghee
juice of 1 lemon, plus wedge to serve
1 tablespoon chopped parsley

01 Preheat oven to 190°C (375°F). Toss oil, broccoli and chilli flakes on a lined baking tray, then season. Bake for 15–20 minutes, until tender but still with a bit of crunch. Combine both flours in a bowl. Season cod and coat with flour mix, shaking off excess. Heat ghee in a frying pan over medium–high heat until bubbling. Add cod, reduce heat and cook for 3–5 minutes on each side. Transfer to a plate. Remove pan from heat and add lemon juice and parsley and stir. Spoon sauce over cod. Serve with broccoli and lemon. Save other fillet for Day 10's lunch.

Nutrition per serving:
942 cals / 66 g fat / 20 g carbs / 7 g fibre / 13 g net carbs / 68 g protein

DINNER
Smoky chilli

SERVINGS: 4
PREP / COOK TIME
15 minutes / 1½ hours

3 tablespoons avocado oil
salt and pepper
900 g (2 lb) beef chuck (braising) steak, cut into 1.5 cm (½ in) chunks
½ onion (60 g / 2 oz), chopped
2 garlic cloves, very finely chopped
1 teaspoon ground cumin
1 teaspoon dried oregano
1 teaspoon very finely chopped chipotle chilli in adobo sauce
400 g (14 oz) tin tomatoes, crushed
½ chicken stock cube
sour cream, grated cheddar, chopped red onion, coriander (cilantro), to serve

01 Heat a large pan and add 2 tablespoons oil. Season beef and, working in batches, brown on all sides. Remove, add remaining oil to pan with onion and garlic and stir for 3–5 minutes. Add cumin, oregano, chilli and tomatoes and stir for 3–5 minutes. Add 480 ml (16 fl oz) water, stock cube and beef. Cover and simmer for 1 hour. Season. Serve with sour cream, cheese, red onion and coriander. Freeze leftovers for another meal.

Nutrition per serving without toppings:
674 cals / 42 g fat / 9.9 g carbs / 2.4 g fibre / 7.5 g net carbs / 62.7 g protein

BLACKBERRY PORRIDGE

COD À LA MEUNIÈRE

SMOKY CHILLI

TUESDAY

If you can't find fresh porcini mushrooms to use in today's dinner, use rehydrated dried porcini instead.

BREAKFAST
Granola & berries

SERVINGS: 1
PREP / COOK TIME
5 minutes / 0 minutes

240 ml (8 fl oz) almond milk
4 tablespoons full-fat Greek yoghurt
20 g (¾ oz) Coconut Flax Granola (p. 172)
20 g (¾ oz) mixed raspberries and
  blackberries

01 Place milk and yoghurt in a bowl and stir until combined. Top with granola and mixed berries.

Nutrition per serving:
229 cals / 20 g fat / 11.3 g carbs /
3.3 g fibre / 8 g net carbs / 6 g protein

LUNCH
Greek salad with feta

SERVINGS: 1
PREP / COOK TIME
5 minutes / 0 minutes

100 g (3½ oz) cos (romaine) lettuce, cut
  into bite-sized pieces
1 short cucumber, sliced
15 g (½ oz) Kalamata olives, pitted
  and halved
¼ red onion, sliced
30 g (1 oz) pepperoncini peppers, sliced
45 g (1½ oz) feta, crumbled
3 tablespoons extra virgin olive oil
1½ tablespoons red wine vinegar
salt and pepper
¼ teaspoon dried oregano, to garnish

01 Arrange lettuce on a plate or in a container. Top with remaining ingredients and drizzle with oil and vinegar. Season with salt and pepper and sprinkle with oregano.

Nutrition per serving:
558 cals / 54 g fat / 13.9 g carbs /
4.7 g fibre / 9.2 g net carbs / 8 g protein

DINNER
Eggplant porcini burgers

SERVINGS: 6
PREP / COOK TIME
15 minutes / 45 minutes

1 large eggplant (aubergine) (670 g/
  1½ lb), chopped
1 red bell pepper (capsicum), chopped
3 tablespoons avocado oil
80 g (2¾ oz) porcini mushrooms, diced
1 garlic clove
60 g (2 oz) almond flour
3 tablespoons grated parmesan
salt and pepper
6 butter (bibb) lettuce leaves
Avocado Oil Mayo and Smoky Tomato
  Jam (p. 74), to serve

01 Preheat oven to 200°C (400°F). Toss eggplant and bell pepper in 2 tablespoons oil and bake for 30 minutes. Cool, then finely chop roasted vegetables, mushroom and garlic in a food processor, then mix with flour and parmesan. Season. Shape into six patties. Cook patties in remaining oil for 3–4 minutes. Serve in lettuce with condiments. Chill leftovers for 4–5 days.

Nutrition per serving:
230 cals / 19 g fat / 13.4 g carbs /
5.1 g fibre / 8.3 g net carbs / 4 g protein

GRANOLA & BERRIES

GREEK SALAD WITH FETA

EGGPLANT PORCINI BURGERS

10

WEDNESDAY

Ground macadamia nuts and shredded coconut make a great keto-friendly crumb for the prawns in today's stir-fry.

BREAKFAST

Lemon poppy seed pancakes

SERVINGS: 4
PREP / COOK TIME
10 minutes / 5 minutes

1 x quantity Keto Pancake Base mix (p. 88)
grated zest from 2 lemons
10 g (⅓ oz) poppy seeds
2 tablespoons ghee

01 Combine pancake mix, lemon zest and poppy seeds in a bowl until well combined. Heat a griddle or frying pan over medium heat and add 1 tablespoon ghee. Pour one-quarter batter into pan and cook until bubbles form on top and the bottom browns, about 2–3 minutes. Flip and cook until second side is browned. Repeat with remaining ghee and batter. Freeze any remaining pancakes for another day.

Nutrition per serving:
417 cals / 36 g fat / 12.7 g carbs /
6.4 g fibre / 6.3 g net carbs / 11.5 g protein

LUNCH

Dark, leafy greens & cod

SERVINGS: 1
PREP / COOK TIME
15 minutes / 0 minutes

25 g (1 oz) kale, shredded
20 g (¾ oz) spring greens, shredded
50 g (1¾ oz) rainbow carrots, shaved into ribbons
1 cod fillet (from Cod à la Meunière, p. 120)
2 tablespoons flaked almonds
60 ml (¼ cup) Avocado Lime Dressing (p. 76)
salt and pepper

01 Arrange greens and carrots on a platter or in a container. Top with cod and almonds. Drizzle over dressing and season to taste.

Nutrition per serving:
544 cals / 38.4 g fat / 13.9 g carbs /
6.3 g fibre / 7.6 g net carbs / 40.2 g protein

DINNER

Coconut prawns & curried vegetables

SERVINGS: 1
PREP / COOK TIME
20 minutes / 25–30 minutes

140 g (5 oz) prawns (shrimp), peeled and deveined
salt and pepper
40 g (1½ oz) ground macadamias (p. 72)
1 egg, whisked
10 g (⅓ oz) shredded coconut
2 tablespoons coconut oil
2 spring onions (scallions), thinly sliced
45 g (1½ oz) broccoli, chopped
1 tablespoon curry powder
60 ml (¼ cup) tinned coconut milk
1 tablespoon tamari

01 Preheat oven to 220°C (430°F). Season prawns, then dip them in ground nuts, egg, then coconut. Place prawns on a baking tray in single layer. Drizzle with 1 tablespoon oil and bake for 8–10 minutes. Heat remaining oil in a pan and stir-fry 1 spring onion. Add broccoli and lightly toss. Add remaining ingredients and 60 ml (¼ cup) water and stir. Cover and cook for 10 minutes. Serve prawns with vegetables.

Nutrition per serving:
527 cals / 47 g fat / 16.4 g carbs /
10.3 g fibre / 6.1 g net carbs / 15 g protein

LEMON POPPY SEED PANCAKES

DARK, LEAFY GREENS & COD

**COCONUT PRAWNS &
CURRIED VEGETABLES**

11

THURSDAY

The mackerel in today's dinner is a great choice when it comes to fish — it's high in fat and omega-3 fatty acids.

BREAKFAST

Cinnamon 'oat'meal

SERVINGS: 1
PREP / COOK TIME
5 minutes / 5 minutes

1 serving Keto 'Oat'meal Base (p. 86)
1 teaspoon ground cinnamon, plus extra to garnish
1 tablespoon roasted pumpkin seeds

01 Combine 'oat'meal base and cinnamon in a pan over medium heat, stirring constantly, for 3–5 minutes. Add pumpkin seeds and sprinkle extra cinnamon on top to garnish.

Nutrition per serving:
461 cals / 37 g fat / 19.3 g carbs / 12.3 g fibre / 7 g net carbs / 17.6 g protein

LUNCH

Summer zoodle salad with chicken

SERVINGS: 1
PREP / COOK TIME
5 minutes / 10 minutes

1 tablespoon almond butter
1 spring onion (scallion), thinly sliced
1 teaspoon lime juice
1 tablespoon coconut aminos or tamari
1 teaspoon monkfruit sweetener
1 teaspoon salt
2 tablespoons coriander (cilantro), leaves chopped, plus extra to garnish
85 g (3 oz) Zoodles (p. 68)
20 g (¾ oz) red cabbage, shredded
170 g (6 oz) chicken thigh fillets, skinless, grilled (broiled) and sliced
salt and pepper

01 Pulse almond butter, onion, lime juice, aminos, sweetener, salt and coriander in a food processor until smooth, adding water if necessary. Drizzle half dressing over zoodles and cabbage. Top with chicken and coriander to garnish. Add more dressing and season.

Nutrition per serving:
428 cals / 19 g fat / 14.8 g carbs / 4.6 g fibre / 10.2 g net carbs / 54 g protein

DINNER

Japanese grilled mackerel with roasted radishes

SERVINGS: 1
PREP / COOK TIME
1 hour 15 minutes / 30 minutes

170 g (6 oz) mackerel fillet
15 ml (½ fl oz) sake
salt and pepper
15 g (½ oz) radishes, halved
2 teaspoons extra virgin olive oil
½ teaspoon toasted sesame seeds
1 teaspoon toasted sesame oil
2 lemon wedges
50 g (1¾ oz) Cauli-rice (p. 72), to serve

01 Combine mackerel, sake and ½ teaspoon salt and chill for 1 hour. Preheat oven to 220°C (430°F). Coat radishes with olive oil, then season. Roast for 15 minutes or until tender. Transfer to a plate. Preheat grill (broiler), then grill (broil) mackerel for 5–8 minutes, until cooked through. Serve with roasted radishes, sesame seeds, sesame oil and lemon, and with cauli-rice on the side.

Nutrition per serving:
366 cals / 19 g fat / 4.8 g carbs / 0.4 g fibre / 4.4 g net carbs / 34.5 g protein

CINNAMON 'OAT' MEAL

SUMMER ZOODLE SALAD WITH CHICKEN

JAPANESE GRILLED MACKEREL WITH ROASTED RADISHES

DAY
12

FRIDAY

There are a number of ways to prepare the zucchini (courgette) for today's dinner. Check out pages 68–70 for an overview of methods and instructions.

BREAKFAST
Matcha kefir-chia pudding

SERVINGS:1
PREP / COOK TIME
1 hour–overnight / 0 minutes

120 ml (4 fl oz) kefir
1 tablespoon chia seeds
1 tablespoon matcha (green tea) powder
2 tablespoons almond milk
1 tablespoon MCT oil
1 tablespoon toasted shredded coconut
1 strawberry, sliced

01 Place kefir, chia seeds, matcha, milk and oil in a jar and stir together to combine. Leave in fridge for at least 1 hour, or overnight. When ready to serve, top with shredded coconut and sliced strawberry.

Nutrition per serving:
326 cals / 25 g fat / 17.9 g carbs / 9.3 g fibre / 8.6 g net carbs / 10.7 g protein

LUNCH
Spring green prawn wraps

SERVINGS: 1
PREP / COOK TIME
15 minutes / 10 minutes

salt and pepper
140 g (5 oz) prawns (shrimp), peeled, deveined and split in half
2 tablespoons extra virgin olive oil
1 teaspoon chipotle chilli powder
2 large spring green leaves, tough rib shaved off
2 tablespoons Garlic Aioli (p. 82)
2 short cucumbers, julienned
1 spring onion (scallion), sliced
3 tablespoons chopped coriander (cilantro)

01 Preheat oven to 180°C (350°F). Season prawns and toss in oil and chipotle. Place prawns on a lined baking tray and bake for 8–10 minutes, until opaque. Set aside. Place 2 spring green leaves on work surface, making 1 large 30 x 13 cm (12 x 5 in) piece. Spread 1 tablespoon aioli down middle of wrap, add prawns and remaining ingredients. Carefully and tightly roll wrap (p. 119), then slice into 2 pieces. Serve with remaining aioli.

Nutrition per serving:
646 cals / 52 g fat / 16.8 g carbs / 9.3 g fibre / 7.5 g net carbs / 38.6 g protein

DINNER
Zucchini cacio e pepe

SERVINGS: 1
PREP / COOK TIME
10 minutes / 5 minutes

2 tablespoons unsalted butter, cubed
100 g (3½ oz) Zoodles (p. 68)
25 g (1 oz) pecorino, grated
3 tablespoons grated parmesan
½ teaspoon freshly ground black pepper

01 Heat 1 tablespoon butter in a frying pan over medium heat. Add zoodles and cheeses and quickly toss. Add remaining butter and black pepper and toss together. Serve.

Nutrition per serving:
404 cals / 36 g fat / 9.2 g carbs / 1 g fibre / 8.2 g net carbs / 14 g protein

MATCHA KEFIR-CHIA PUDDING

SPRING GREEN PRAWN WRAPS

ZUCCHINI CACIO E PEPE

SATURDAY

Using tinned tuna for today's niçoise salad lunch makes prep work a lot easier.

BREAKFAST

Mushroom baked eggs

SERVINGS: 1
PREP / COOK TIME
10 minutes / 20 minutes

3 tablespoons ghee, plus extra for greasing
20 g (¾ oz) onion, sliced
60 g (2 oz) mixed mushrooms, sliced
salt and pepper
2 large eggs
½ avocado, cubed (optional)
3 tablespoons crumbled feta (optional)
1 tablespoon dill fronds (optional)

01 Preheat oven to 190°C (375°F). Grease a ramekin and set aside. Heat ghee in a frying pan over medium–high heat. Add onion and cook until translucent. Add mushrooms and cook until browned. Season. Break an egg into prepared ramekin and add cooked onion and mushrooms, then add other egg on top. Season. Bake for 5–10 minutes until consistency of egg is to your liking. Top with remaining ingredients, if liked, and serve.

Nutrition per serving:
698 cals / 66 g fat / 11.6 g carbs /
5.4 g fibre / 6.2 g net carbs / 20 g protein

LUNCH

Niçoise salad

SERVINGS: 1
PREP / COOK TIME
15 minutes / 0 minutes

100 g (3½ oz) little gem lettuce
85 g (3 oz) green beans, blanched
1 short cucumber, sliced into half moons
50 g (1¾ oz) semi-dried tomatoes, halved
1 egg, hard-boiled (p. 178)
50 g (1¾ oz) radishes, thinly sliced
2 teaspoons capers
1 tablespoon dill fronds
125 g (4½ oz) tinned tuna in oil, drained
  and broken into pieces
60 ml (¼ cup) Avocado Lime Dressing
  (p. 76)
salt and pepper

01 Arrange lettuce in a shallow bowl or container. Top with remaining ingredients. Drizzle with dressing and season with salt and pepper.

Nutrition per serving:
653 cals / 47 g fat / 20.5 g carbs /
10.1 g fibre / 10.4 g net carbs / 43.5 g protein

DINNER

Cast-iron steak with wedge salad

SERVINGS: 1
PREP / COOK TIME
5 minutes / 5–10 minutes

salt and pepper
170 g (6 oz) grass-fed oyster blade (flat
  iron) steak, at room temperature for at
  least 30 minutes
2 tablespoons avocado oil
2 tablespoons unsalted butter
1 garlic clove, mashed
1 wedge of iceberg lettuce
45 ml (1½ fl oz) Blue Cheese Dressing
  (p. 76)
1 tablespoon chopped parsley, to garnish

01 Season steak. Heat a cast-iron frying pan over high heat until smoking. Add oil to pan, add steak and cook for 3–5 minutes on one side. Turn over and cook for another 3–5 minutes, until medium–rare. Turn off heat, add butter and garlic and lightly baste steak with mix. Serve steak with lettuce and dressing. Garnish with parsley.

Nutrition per serving:
971 cals / 88.3 g fat / 8.7 g carbs /
5.1 g fibre / 3.6 g net carbs / 37.1 g protein

MUSHROOM BAKED EGGS

NIÇOISE SALAD

CAST-IRON STEAK WITH WEDGE SALAD

DAY

14

SUNDAY

When making today's curried kale soup, be sure to use a low-carb stock.

BREAKFAST

Poached eggs with burrata, asparagus & roasted tomatoes

SERVINGS: 1
PREP / COOK TIME
5 minutes / 10–15 minutes

100 g (3½ oz) asparagus spears
135 g (5 oz) cherry tomatoes
2 tablespoons extra virgin olive oil
1 tablespoon thyme leaves
salt and pepper
2 eggs, poached
30 g (1 oz) burrata

01 Preheat oven to 180°C (350°F). Toss asparagus and tomatoes with oil, thyme and salt and pepper. Roast for 10–15 minutes, until asparagus is cooked and tomatoes are roasted. Arrange asparagus on a plate, add poached eggs, burrata and tomatoes. Season.

Nutrition per serving:
527 cals / 45.1 g fat / 9.9 g carbs /
3.3 g fibre / 6.6 g net carbs / 20.8 g protein

LUNCH

Cabbage steak tacos

SERVINGS: 1
PREP / COOK TIME
15 minutes / 15–20 minutes

2 tablespoons Taco Seasoning (p. 80)
3 tablespoons avocado oil
115 g (4 oz) grass-fed oyster blade
  (flat iron) steak
30 g (1 oz) onion, sliced
½ jalapeno, sliced into thin rings
25 g (1 oz) grated cheddar
½ avocado, diced
2 tablespoons chopped coriander (cilantro)
2 whole red cabbage leaves
salt and pepper
lime wedges, to serve

01 Combine taco seasoning and 2 tablespoons oil in a large bowl and add steak. Marinate for 10–15 minutes. Heat a frying pan over medium–high heat. Add remaining oil and onion and cook until translucent. Remove onion from pan and set aside. Increase heat to high, add steak and cook for 3–5 minutes on each side until medium–rare. Rest, then slice. Assemble cabbage tacos, using cabbage as 'shells'. Add steak to cabbage along with remaining ingredients. Season. Serve with lime wedges.

Nutrition per serving:
812 cals / 68 g fat / 22.2 g carbs /
8 g fibre / 14.2 g net carbs / 31 g protein

DINNER

Curried kale soup

SERVINGS: 6
PREP / COOK TIME
15 minutes / 1 hour

2 tablespoons coconut oil
1 teaspoon grated ginger
2 tablespoons curry powder
1 tablespoon ground turmeric
1 tablespoon very finely chopped garlic
1 litre (4 cups) chicken stock from
  low-carb stock cubes
380 ml (13 fl oz) tinned coconut milk
1 teaspoon fish sauce
2 tablespoons tamari
255 g (9 oz) Cauli-rice (p. 72)
8 kale leaves, ribbed and chopped
salt and pepper
4 coriander (cilantro) sprigs
juice of 1 lime

01 Heat oil in a large pan. Add ginger and spices and stir until aromatic. Add garlic and stir, then add stock, coconut milk, fish sauce and tamari. Cover and simmer for 30–45 minutes. Add cauli-rice and kale. Season. Top with coriander and lime and serve. Store remaining soup in fridge for another meal.

Nutrition per serving:
234 cals / 18 g fat / 9.5 g carbs /
6.3 g fibre / 3.2 g net carbs / 8.3 g protein

**POACHED EGGS WITH
BURRATA, ASPARAGUS &
ROASTED TOMATOES**

CABBAGE STEAK TACOS

**CURRIED
KALE SOUP**

WEEK 3
WEEKLY SHOPPING LIST

FRUIT
- [ ] raspberries
- [ ] blackberries
- [ ] strawberries
- [ ] lemon – 3
- [ ] lime – 2
- [ ] orange – 1
- [ ] avocado – 2

VEGETABLES
- [ ] cos (romaine) lettuce – 1 head
- [ ] little gem lettuce – 2
- [ ] mixed greens – 30 g (1 oz)
- [ ] iceberg lettuce – 1 head
- [ ] baby spinach – 15 g (½ oz)
- [ ] kale – 1 bunch
- [ ] spring greens – 400 g (14 oz)
- [ ] beetroot (beets) – 3
- [ ] tomato – 1 medium
- [ ] carrots – 1
- [ ] short cucumber – 3
- [ ] brown onion – 2 small
- [ ] white onion – 1 small
- [ ] red onion – 1 small
- [ ] spring onions (scallions) – 1 bunch
- [ ] shallot – 4
- [ ] garlic – 1 bulb
- [ ] ginger – 1 large piece
- [ ] rainbow carrots – 1 bunch
- [ ] celery – 1 small bunch
- [ ] radishes – 1 bunch
- [ ] zucchini (courgettes) – 3
- [ ] cauliflower – 1 small head
- [ ] spaghetti squash – 2 large
- [ ] parsley, coriander (cilantro), dill, thyme, chives, basil – 1 bunch each
- [ ] jalapeno chilli – 1
- [ ] red chilli – 1

PROTEINS
- [ ] chicken breast – 2 x 115 g (4 oz)
- [ ] chicken thighs, bone in, skin on – 225 g (8 oz)
- [ ] pork shoulder – 900 g (2 lb)
- [ ] grass-fed fillet (tenderloin) steak – 170 g (6 oz)
- [ ] ham – 260 g (9 oz)
- [ ] pork fillet (tenderloin) – 450 g (1 lb)
- [ ] minced (ground) beef – 225 g (8 oz)
- [ ] chicken livers – 450 g (1 lb)
- [ ] lardons, fat only – 2 tablespoons

DAIRY/EGGS
- [ ] double (heavy) cream
- [ ] almond milk
- [ ] full-fat Greek yoghurt
- [ ] ricotta
- [ ] labneh
- [ ] unsalted butter
- [ ] cream cheese – 115 g (4 oz)
- [ ] queso fresco or feta – 220 g (8 oz)
- [ ] parmesan – 100 g (3½ oz)
- [ ] haloumi – 435 g (15½ oz)
- [ ] blue cheese – 2 tablespoons
- [ ] eggs – 24

MISC
- [ ] pico de gallo
- [ ] kelp noodles
- [ ] red wine

CHECK TO SEE IF IN PANTRY
- [ ] extra virgin olive oil
- [ ] avocado oil
- [ ] ghee
- [ ] MCT oil
- [ ] coconut oil
- [ ] apple cider vinegar
- [ ] white wine vinegar

- [ ] whole tomatoes, tin – 400 g (14 oz)
- [ ] diced tomatoes, tin – 400 g (14 oz)
- [ ] passata (pureed tomatoes)
- [ ] roasted red peppers (capsicums) – 1 jar
- [ ] anchovy fillets in oil
- [ ] soy sauce
- [ ] tahini
- [ ] flaked almonds
- [ ] brazil nuts
- [ ] macadamia nuts
- [ ] walnuts – 30 g (1 oz)
- [ ] chia seeds
- [ ] psyllium husk
- [ ] hemp seeds
- [ ] ground cinnamon
- [ ] ground cumin
- [ ] curry powder
- [ ] dried bay leaves
- [ ] chilli flakes
- [ ] chipotle chilli powder
- [ ] smoked paprika
- [ ] aleppo pepper
- [ ] ground ginger
- [ ] star anise
- [ ] coconut flour
- [ ] almond flour
- [ ] arrowroot or cornflour (corn starch)
- [ ] baking powder
- [ ] baking soda
- [ ] natural vanilla extract
- [ ] shredded coconut
- [ ] sukrin gold
- [ ] tinned artichoke hearts
- [ ] black olives, pitted
- [ ] capers
- [ ] Dijon mustard

WEEK 3 PREP

Check to see if you have any of these basics already made and if not, add ingredients to your shopping list.

BASICS
(these are items that you should have pre-prepped as they will last a while)

☐ Taco Seasoning (p. 80)
☐ Pickling Liquid (p. 72)
☐ Smoky Tomato Jam (p. 74)
☐ Coconut Butter (p. 74)
☐ Keto Pancake Base mix (p. 88)
☐ Dukkah blend (p. 182)
☐ Seeded Keto Bread (p. 84)
   (unless you have frozen)

PREP
☐ Zucchini ribbons (p.68) for Zucchini Fettuccine Alfredo with Chicken (p. 138)
☐ Zoodles (p. 68)
☐ Grind macadamias for Cauliflower Fritters (p. 148)
☐ Chicken breast for Curried Chicken Salad (p. 140)

MAKE
☐ Zucchini Bread (p. 142)
☐ Coconut Berry Chia Parfait (p. 144)
☐ Avocado Oil Mayo (p. 74)

☐ Avocado Lime Dressing (p. 76)
☐ Tahini Herb Dressing (p. 76)
☐ Beetroot Dip (p. 182)
☐ Tzatziki (p. 78)
☐ Chicken Liver Mousse (p. 182)
☐ Curried Chicken Salad (p. 140)

ROAST
☐ Spaghetti squash for Spaghetti Squash Bowls (p. 142) and Puttanesca Spaghetti Squash (p. 146)
☐ Roast beetroot (beets) for Beetroot Dip (p. 182)

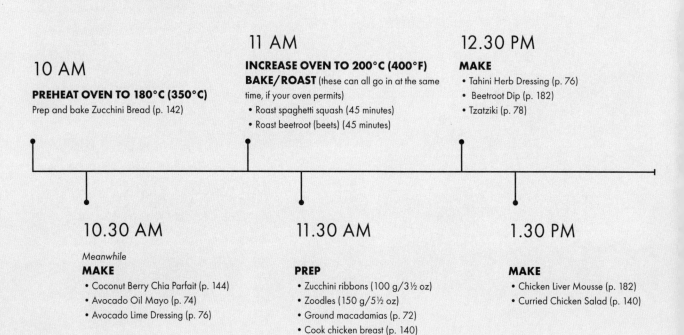

WEEK 3 TIMETABLE

10 AM
PREHEAT OVEN TO 180°C (350°C)
Prep and bake Zucchini Bread (p. 142)

11 AM
INCREASE OVEN TO 200°C (400°F)
BAKE/ROAST (these can all go in at the same time, if your oven permits)
• Roast spaghetti squash (45 minutes)
• Roast beetroot (beets) (45 minutes)

12.30 PM
MAKE
• Tahini Herb Dressing (p. 76)
• Beetroot Dip (p. 182)
• Tzatziki (p. 78)

10.30 AM
Meanwhile
MAKE
• Coconut Berry Chia Parfait (p. 144)
• Avocado Oil Mayo (p. 74)
• Avocado Lime Dressing (p. 76)

11.30 AM
PREP
• Zucchini ribbons (100 g/3½ oz)
• Zoodles (150 g/5½ oz)
• Ground macadamias (p. 72)
• Cook chicken breast (p. 140)

1.30 PM
MAKE
• Chicken Liver Mousse (p. 182)
• Curried Chicken Salad (p. 140)

PREPARING & STEAMING ARTICHOKES

1. Cut off excess stem

2. Cut off tips of leaves and slice off top

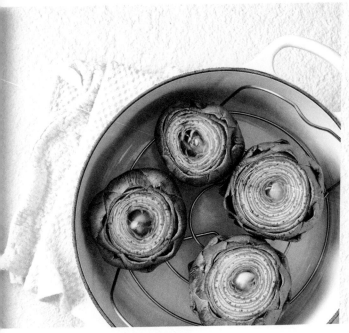

3. Place in steamer basket in pot of water

4. Cover and steam for 20–40 minutes, until artichoke hearts are tender

DAY

15

MONDAY

Today's zucchini fettuccine lunch can be prepared the night before and reheated when you are ready to eat, for an easy takeaway meal.

BREAKFAST

Berry ricotta pancakes

SERVINGS: 1
PREP / COOK TIME
10 minutes / 15 minutes

1 serving Keto Pancake Base mix (p. 88)
60 g (¼ cup) ricotta
¼ teaspoon natural vanilla extract
15 g (½ oz) raspberries, halved
1 tablespoon ghee

01 Combine pancake mix, ricotta and vanilla in a bowl until thoroughly combined. Fold in raspberries. Heat griddle or frying pan and add ghee. Pour batter into pan into size of pancake desired. Flip pancakes when bubbles form on top and bottom browns, about 2–3 minutes. Cook until second side is browned. Repeat and serve.

Nutrition per serving:
454 cals / 36 g fat / 15.5 g carbs / 6.8 g fibre / 8.7 g net carbs / 18 g protein

LUNCH

Zucchini fettuccine alfredo with chicken

SERVINGS: 1
PREP / COOK TIME
15 minutes / 15 minutes

¼ teaspoon arrowroot or cornflour (corn starch)
1 small garlic clove, grated
1 tablespoon unsalted butter
50 g (½ cup) grated parmesan
40 ml (1¼ fl oz) double (heavy) cream
salt and pepper
100 g (3½ oz) zucchini (courgette) ribbons
2 tinned artichoke hearts, halved
115 g (4 oz) chicken breast, cooked and sliced
parsley leaves, to garnish

01 Place 70 ml (2¼ fl oz) water in a large frying pan over medium heat. Add arrowroot and whisk until dissolved. Bring water to a low simmer. Add garlic and butter and melt. Add cheese and whisk to incorporate. Add cream and a pinch of salt and whisk. Add zucchini and artichoke and toss for 1–2 minutes. Serve, topped with chicken and parsley. Season.

Nutrition per serving:
906 cals / 68 g fat / 13.3 g carbs / 4.3 g fibre / 9 g net carbs / 64.7 g protein

DINNER

Carnitas

SERVINGS: 2–4
PREP / COOK TIME
15 minutes / 6–8 hours

900 g (2 lb) pork shoulder, fat trimmed
salt and pepper
3 teaspoons Taco Seasoning (p. 80)
¼ teaspoon chipotle chilli powder
2 strips orange peel
3 garlic cloves, very finely chopped
½ white onion, chopped, plus extra finely chopped to garnish
1 dried bay leaf
cos (romaine) lettuce, coriander (cilantro) and pico de gallo, to serve

01 Season pork shoulder with 2 teaspoons salt and pepper. Rub pork shoulder with taco seasoning and chipotle powder. Place pork in slow cooker along with orange peel, garlic, onion and bay leaf. Cook on low for 6–8 hours, until pork is tender. Shred pork and serve on lettuce leaves topped with coriander and pico de gallo. Store left-over carnitas mixture in fridge for lunch on day 17.

Nutrition per serving:
611 cals / 35 g fat / 9.1 g carbs / 2.2 g fibre / 6.9 g net carbs / 63 g protein

BERRY RICOTTA PANCAKES

**ZUCCHINI FETTUCCINE
ALFREDO WITH CHICKEN**

CARNITAS

DAY

16

TUESDAY

Frozen seeded bread is great for making a quick meal, like topping it with chicken salad for today's lunch. Simply thaw a couple of slices when you're ready to eat.

BREAKFAST

Berry smoothie bowl

SERVINGS: 1
PREP / COOK TIME
5 minutes / 0 minutes

60 ml (¼ cup) almond milk
2 tablespoons full-fat Greek yoghurt
½ avocado
1 tablespoon MCT oil
25 g (1 oz) raspberries
25 g (1 oz) blackberries
10 g (⅓ oz) brazil nuts, chopped

01 Place milk, yoghurt and avocado in a blender along with 250 g (9 oz) ice. With the motor running, slowly add oil. Pour into a bowl and top with berries and nuts. Serve immediately.

Nutrition per serving:
363 cals / 96 g fat / 26.8 g carbs /
16.4 g fibre / 10.4 g net carbs / 54 g protein

LUNCH

Curried chicken salad on seeded bread

SERVINGS: 1
PREP / COOK TIME
15 minutes / 0 minutes

3 tablespoons Avocado Oil Mayo (p. 74)
2 teaspoons curry powder
115 g (4 oz) chicken breast, cooked and shredded
1 celery stalk, diced
1 spring onion (scallion), sliced
15 g (½ oz) flaked almonds, toasted
salt and pepper
2 slices Seeded Keto Bread (p. 84), to serve

01 Mix mayo and curry powder together in a bowl until well combined. Fold in remaining ingredients. Season. Serve with bread. The chicken salad can be made up to 3 days in advance and stored in fridge.

Nutrition per serving:
1119 cals / 94 g fat / 21.2 g carbs /
13.8 g fibre / 7.4 g net carbs / 53 g protein

DINNER

Dukkah beef with Mediterranean plate

SERVINGS: 1
PREP / COOK TIME
15 minutes / 5–10 minutes

170 g (6 oz) grass-fed fillet (tenderloin) steak
salt and pepper
2 tablespoons Dukkah blend (p. 182)
2 tablespoons avocado oil
60 g (2 oz) labneh
1 short cucumber, sliced into spears
4 radishes, halved or quartered
2 haloumi slices, grilled

01 Coat steak with 1 ½ teaspoons salt and pepper and the dukkah blend, then set aside. Heat chargrill pan over high heat until smoking. Add oil and steak and cook for 3–5 minutes on each side or until cooked to your liking. Serve steak with labneh, vegetables and haloumi.

Nutrition per serving:
1081 cals / 91 g fat / 15.9 g carbs /
7.1 g fibre / 8.8 g net carbs / 62.8 g protein

BERRY SMOOTHIE BOWL

**CURRIED CHICKEN SALAD
ON SEEDED BREAD**

**DUKKAH BEEF WITH
MEDITERRANEAN PLATE**

— DAY — 17

WEDNESDAY

Zucchini bread freezes very well. Cut it into slices after today's breakfast and freeze in a zip-lock bag for up to a month.

BREAKFAST

Zucchini bread with coconut butter

SERVINGS: 12
PREP / COOK TIME
30 minutes / 45–60 minutes

140 g (5 oz) zucchini (courgette), grated
2 teaspoons salt
60 g (2 oz) coconut flour
10 g (⅓ oz) almond flour
90 g (3 oz) sukrin gold
1 tablespoon psyllium husk
1 teaspoon baking powder
½ teaspoon baking soda
1½ teaspoons ground cinnamon
5 eggs
115 g (4 oz) coconut oil
1 tablespoon Coconut Butter (p. 74),
  to serve

01 Preheat oven to 180°C (350°C). Oil and line a loaf (bar) tin. Salt zucchini with 1 teaspoon salt. Leave for 10 minutes, then wring out excess moisture. Combine dry ingredients with rest of salt. In another bowl, mix eggs and oil together. Add dry ingredients and zucchini and mix well. Pour into tin and bake for 45–60 minutes. Serve with coconut butter.

Nutrition per serving:
282 cals / 26 g fat / 9.2 g carbs /
5.6 g fibre / 3.6 g net carbs / 5 g protein

LUNCH

Little gem salad with left-over carnitas

SERVINGS: 1
PREP / COOK TIME
15 minutes / 0 minutes

100 g (3½ oz) little gem lettuces
1 red chilli (or jalapeno), sliced
150 g (5½ oz) left-over Carnitas (p. 138)
2 tablespoons crumbled queso fresco
  or feta
95 ml (3¼ fl oz) Avocado Lime Dressing
  (p. 76)
salt and pepper

01 Arrange little gem lettuces in a shallow bowl or container. Top with remaining ingredients and drizzle over dressing. Season.

Nutrition per serving:
670 cals / 54 g fat / 12.2 g carbs /
4.4 g fibre / 7.8 g net carbs / 35.8 g protein

DINNER

Spaghetti squash bowls

SERVINGS: 6
PREP / COOK TIME
15 minutes / 0 minutes

2 shallots, sliced
60 ml (¼ cup) Pickling Liquid (p. 72)
65 g (2¼ oz) kale, chopped
2 tablespoons extra virgin olive oil
3 thyme sprigs, leaves chopped
salt and pepper
½ roasted spaghetti squash (155 g/
  5½ oz) (p. 101)
245 g (8½ oz) ham, chopped
180 g (6½ oz) queso fresco or feta,
  crumbled

01 Combine shallot and pickling liquid in a bowl and leave for 10 minutes. Massage kale with oil and thyme, then season. Meanwhile, scrape squash interior, being careful to keep skin intact. Stir all ingredients, except cheese, into squash with squash 'noodles'. Season and top with cheese. Store any remaining filling in fridge for another meal.

Nutrition per serving:
277 cals / 21 g fat / 9.2 g carbs / 1.9 g fibre /
7.3 g net carbs / 15 g protein

ZUCCHINI BREAD WITH COCONUT BUTTER

LITTLE GEM SALAD WITH LEFT-OVER CARNITAS

SPAGHETTI SQUASH BOWLS

DAY

18

THURSDAY

If you like to eat snacks for a meal, today's crudité dinner will be especially appealing (and quick to prepare, too!).

BREAKFAST

Coconut berry chia parfait

SERVINGS: 1
PREP / COOK TIME
1 hour–overnight / 0 minutes

120 ml (4 fl oz) almond milk
1 tablespoon chia seeds
1 tablespoon hemp seeds
2 tablespoons full-fat Greek yoghurt
1 tablespoon MCT oil
1 strawberry, sliced
25 g (1 oz) raspberries
25 g (1 oz) blackberries
1 tablespoon toasted shredded coconut

01 Place milk, chia seeds, hemp seeds, yoghurt and oil in a bowl and stir together. Leave in fridge for at least 1 hour, or overnight. Layer chia pudding and some berries, then top with coconut and remaining berries.

Nutrition per serving:
329 cals / 28 g fat / 14.5 g carbs /
7.8 g fibre / 6.7 g net carbs / 9 g protein

LUNCH

Mediterranean salad

SERVINGS: 1
PREP / COOK TIME
15 minutes / 15 minutes

15 g (½ oz) kale, chopped
30 g (1 oz) mixed leaves
2 radishes, sliced
40 g (1½ oz) red onion, sliced
4 slices haloumi, griddled
4 pitted black olives, halved
45 ml (1½ fl oz) Tahini Herb Dressing
  (p. 76)
salt and pepper

01 Arrange kale and mixed greens in a shallow bowl or container. Top with remaining ingredients, drizzle with dressing, then season.

Nutrition per serving:
741 cals / 64 g fat / 12.8 g carbs /
3.1 g fibre / 9.7 g net carbs / 32 g protein

DINNER

Crudité plate (with assorted dips, cheese & charcuterie)

SERVINGS: 1
PREP / COOK TIME
15 minutes / 0 minutes

80 g (2¾ oz) Chicken Liver Mousse
  (p. 182)
50 g (1¾ oz) Beetroot Dip (p. 182)
3 radishes, quartered or halved
3 slices haloumi, griddled
2 rainbow carrots, sliced into spears
2 celery stalks, sliced into spears

01 Arrange dips in small bowls on a platter. Arrange vegetables and cheese on the platter and serve.

Nutrition per serving:
733 cals / 60 g fat / 14.4 g carbs /
4.7 g fibre / 9.7 g net carbs / 35.5 g protein

COCONUT BERRY
CHIA PARFAIT

MEDITERRANEAN SALAD

CRUDITÉ PLATE (WITH
ASSORTED DIPS, CHEESE
& CHARCUTERIE)

DAY

19

FRIDAY

Eggs, like the coddled one in today's breakfast, are very nutritious in addition to being a reliable, keto-friendly ingredient.

BREAKFAST

Coddled egg with ham & seeded bread

SERVINGS: 1
PREP / COOK TIME
10 minutes / 8–10 minutes

1 tablespoon unsalted butter
60 ml (¼ cup) double (heavy) cream
15 g (½ oz) baby spinach
1 tablespoon diced ham
1 teaspoon chives
1 egg
salt and pepper
1 slice Seeded Keto Bread (p. 84), to serve

01 Place a small 120 ml (4 fl oz) jar with a lid in a pan and fill with water three-quarters of the way up jar. Remove jar and bring water to a simmer. Butter inside jar and pour in 30 ml (1 fl oz) cream. Add spinach, ham and chives to jar, then break egg on top. Pour in remaining cream, season and seal jar. Place jar in simmering water and simmer for 8–10 minutes, until egg white is opaque. Serve immediately with bread.

Nutrition per serving:
534 cals / 50 g fat / 9.3 g carbs /
5.7 g fibre / 3.6 g net carbs / 16 g protein

LUNCH

Chicken zoodle soup

SERVINGS: 2
PREP / COOK TIME
15 minutes / 1 hour

2 tablespoons extra virgin olive oil
½ small onion (35 g / 1¼ oz), diced
1 carrot, diced
1 celery stalk, diced
1 dried bay leaf
½ teaspoon chopped thyme leaves
225 g (8 oz) chicken thighs, bone in and skin on
juice of ½ lemon
salt and pepper
150 g (5½ oz) Zoodles (p. 68)

01 Heat oil in a pan, add onion, carrot and celery and cook until onion is translucent. Add herbs and chicken and cook for 5 minutes until chicken is lightly browned. Add 1.5 litres (6 cups) water, cover and bring to the boil. Reduce heat, cover and simmer for 45 minutes. Remove chicken from soup and shred meat off bone. Return meat to soup, squeeze in lemon and season. Divide zoodles into bowls and add piping hot soup, which will lightly cook zoodles. Serve. Store any remaining in fridge for another meal.

Nutrition per serving:
295 cals / 20 g fat / 9.9 g carbs /
2.8 g fibre / 7.1 g net carbs / 21 g protein

DINNER

Puttanesca spaghetti squash

SERVINGS: 3–4
PREP / COOK TIME
10 minutes / 15–20 minutes

2 tablespoons extra virgin olive oil
2 garlic cloves, very finely chopped
2 anchovy fillets
1½ teaspoons chilli flakes
400 g (14 oz) tin whole roma (plum) tomatoes, crushed
salt and pepper
3 tablespoons pitted black olives
1 tablespoon capers
465 g (1 lb) spaghetti squash, roasted and shredded (p. 101)
basil, to garnish

01 Heat oil in a pan over medium heat and add garlic, anchovy fillets and chilli flakes. With a wooden spoon, break anchovies apart. Add tomatoes and season. Increase heat to medium–high and cook for 10 minutes. Stir in olives and capers and cook for 2–3 minutes. Toss squash 'noodles' with sauce, then garnish with basil. Store any remaining in fridge for another meal.

Nutrition per serving:
156 cals / 10 g fat / 16.4 g carbs /
3.4 g fibre / 13 g net carbs / 3 g protein

CODDLED EGG WITH HAM & SEEDED BREAD

CHICKEN ZOODLE SOUP

PUTTANESCA SPAGHETTI SQUASH

20

SATURDAY

The cauliflower fritters in today's lunch can be made the night before, just cook them up when you are ready to eat lunch.

BREAKFAST

Haloumi & zucchini frittata

SERVINGS: 6
PREP / COOK TIME
15 minutes / 25 minutes

3 tablespoons extra virgin olive oil
2 shallots (90 g/3 oz), thinly sliced
1 large zucchini (courgette), sliced
  into half-moons
165 g (6 oz) haloumi, cubed
8 eggs, whisked
6 dill sprigs, chopped
salt and pepper

01 Preheat oven to 180°C (350°C). Heat oil in a large non-stick, ovenproof frying pan, add shallot and zucchini and cook until shallot is translucent. Add haloumi and cook for 3–5 minutes, until lightly browned. Combine eggs with dill, salt and pepper in a bowl, then pour into pan. Cover for 2–3 minutes, then uncover and bake in oven for 10 minutes, or until cooked through. Slice into 6 pieces to serve. Freeze any remaining pieces for another meal.

Nutrition per serving:
232 cals / 18 g fat / 3.7 g carbs /
0.7 g fibre / 3 g net carbs / 12.9 g protein

LUNCH

Cauliflower fritters with tzatziki

SERVINGS: 1
PREP / COOK TIME
15 minutes / 10 minutes

75 g (2¾ oz) Cauli-rice (p. 72), steamed
  and squeezed dry
1 egg, whisked
1 garlic clove, very finely chopped
50 g (½ cup) finely grated parmesan
70 g (2½ oz) ground macadamias (p. 72)
1 tablespoon chopped parsley leaves
salt and pepper
60 ml (¼ cup) avocado oil
60 ml (¼ cup) Tzatziki (p. 78) and 2 lemon
  wedges, to serve

01 Combine cauli-rice, egg, garlic, parmesan, ground macadamias and parsley in a large bowl, then season. Shape mixture into four fritters. Heat oil in a large frying pan over medium heat and cook fritters for 2–3 minutes on each side. Repeat as necessary. Serve with tzatziki and lemon wedges.

Nutrition per serving:
857 cals / 86 g fat / 13.3 g carbs /
4.4 g fibre / 8.9 g net carbs / 13.5 g protein

DINNER

Tahini pork fillet

SERVINGS: 4
PREP / COOK TIME
15 minutes / 20 minutes

salt and pepper
450 g (1 lb) pork fillet (tenderloin), cut into
  1 cm (½ in) thick slices
1 tablespoon aleppo pepper
1 teaspoon ground ginger
1 teaspoon Dijon mustard
60 ml (¼ cup) avocado oil
400 g (14 oz) spring greens, chopped
170 ml (⅔ cup) Tahini Herb Dressing
  (p. 76)

01 Season the pork fillet slices and set aside. Mix aleppo pepper, ginger and mustard together in a small bowl. Rub mixture over pork. Heat a large frying pan over medium–high heat, add 2 tablespoons oil and once hot, add pork and cook for 5–6 minutes until pork is browned all over. Remove and leave to rest. Add remaining oil to pan, add greens and cook for 5–10 minutes, until tender. Serve pork with greens and dressing, reserving 60 g (2 oz) pork for lunch on p. 150.

Nutrition per serving:
564 cals / 43 g fat / 7.2 g carbs /
3.7 g fibre / 3.5 g net carbs / 36.3 g protein

HALOUMI & ZUCCHINI FRITTATA

**CAULIFLOWER FRITTERS
WITH TZATZIKI**

TAHINI PORK FILLET

— DAY —

21

SUNDAY

Kelp noodles, the base of today's lunch, are a nutritious, low-carb swap for pasta, and are especially great when you don't feel like making zoodles.

BREAKFAST

Smoky tomato baked eggs

SERVINGS: 4–6
PREP / COOK TIME
10 minutes / 15–20 minutes

3 tablespoons ghee
1 small onion, thinly sliced
150 g (5½ oz) roasted red peppers, sliced
½ teaspoon smoked paprika
½ teaspoon ground cumin
400 g (14 oz) tin diced tomatoes
salt and pepper
6 eggs
2 tablespoons feta, crumbled
coriander (cilantro), to garnish

01 Preheat oven to 180°C (350°C). Melt ghee in a large frying pan over medium heat, add onion and red peppers and cook for 5–8 minutes, until onion is translucent and soft. Add spices and stir. Add tomatoes and season. Simmer until thickened. Break each egg into tomato mixture and crumble cheese on top. Bake for 8–10 minutes, until eggs are desired consistency. Season and garnish with coriander. Store any remaining in fridge for another meal.

Nutrition per serving:
196 cals / 15 g fat / 6.7 g carbs /
0.9 g fibre / 5.8 g net carbs / 9.2 g protein

LUNCH

Ginger kelp noodles with left-over pork

SERVINGS: 1
PREP / COOK TIME
15 minutes / 0 minutes

2 tablespoons coconut oil, melted
3 tablespoons thinly sliced ginger
1 tablespoon soy sauce
1 teaspoon sukrin gold
1½ teaspoons passata (pureed tomatoes)
1½ teaspoons apple cider vinegar
115 g (4 oz) kelp noodles
60 g (2 oz) pork fillet (tenderloin) medallions from Tahini Pork Fillet (p. 148), thinly sliced
1 spring onion (scallion), thinly sliced diagonally

01 Blend oil, ginger, soy sauce, sukrin, passata and vinegar in a food processor until smooth. Toss kelp noodles with sauce. Top noodles with pork, then garnish with spring onion to serve.

Nutrition per serving:
385 cals / 31 g fat / 12.9 g carbs /
2.1 g fibre / 10.8 g net carbs / 19.7 g protein

DINNER

Blue cheese burgers in lettuce wraps

SERVINGS: 1
PREP / COOK TIME
15 minutes / 15 minutes

225 g (8 oz) minced (ground) beef
2 tablespoons crumbled blue cheese
salt and pepper
2 tablespoons extra virgin olive oil
4 large iceberg lettuce leaves
2 slices red onion
2 slices tomato
40 g (1½ oz) Smoky Tomato Jam (p. 74)
30 ml (1 fl oz) Avocado Oil Mayo (p. 74)
2 teaspoons Dijon mustard
½ avocado, thinly sliced

01 Combine beef with blue cheese and season, then divide in half and form into two patties. Heat a frying pan or barbecue and add oil (if using pan). Cook burgers until medium–rare, or to your liking. For each burger, place two lettuce leaves overlapping to form a large surface area, then top with a burger and the remaining ingredients and serve.

Nutrition per serving:
664 cals / 56 g fat / 8.8 g carbs /
3.6 g fibre / 5.2 g net carbs / 3.4 g protein

SMOKY TOMATO BAKED EGGS

**GINGER KELP NOODLES
WITH LEFT-OVER PORK**

**BLUE CHEESE BURGERS
IN LETTUCE WRAPS**

WEEK 4
WEEKLY SHOPPING LIST

FRUIT

- [ ] lemon – 5
- [ ] lime – 3
- [ ] avocado – 2

VEGETABLES

- [ ] little gem lettuce – 1 head
- [ ] butter (bibb) lettuce – 1 small head
- [ ] English spinach – 1 small bunch
- [ ] frisee (curly endive) – 1 small head
- [ ] radicchio – ¼ head
- [ ] witlof (Belgian endive/chicory) – 1 head
- [ ] watercress – 1 small bunch
- [ ] green cabbage – 1 small head
- [ ] cavolo nero –1 bunch
- [ ] kale – 1 bunch
- [ ] spring greens – 1 bunch
- [ ] cherry tomatoes – 80 g (2¾ oz)
- [ ] brown onion – 2 medium
- [ ] red onion – 1 small
- [ ] spring onions (scallions) – 1
- [ ] bunch cucumber – 1
- [ ] shallots – 2
- [ ] garlic – 1 bulb
- [ ] ginger – 1 piece
- [ ] carrot – 1
- [ ] celery – 1 small bunch
- [ ] radishes – 1 bunch
- [ ] fennel – 1 bulb
- [ ] zucchini (courgette) – 1
- [ ] green bell pepper (capsicum) – 1
- [ ] jalapeno chilli – 1
- [ ] red chilli (or jalapeno) – 1 small
- [ ] cauliflower – 1 large head
- [ ] Brussels sprouts – 360 g (12½ oz)
- [ ] basil, Thai basil, mint, thyme, chives, parsley, dill, coriander (cilantro) – 1 bunch each
- [ ] lemongrass stalks – 2

PROTEINS

- [ ] 1 whole chicken –1.5 kg (3 lb 5 oz)
- [ ] Scotch fillet (rib eye) steak – 180 g (6½ oz)
- [ ] hanger (skirt) steak – 85 g (3 oz)
- [ ] boneless pork shoulder – 450 g (1 lb)
- [ ] bacon strips – 100 g (3½ oz)
- [ ] ham – 50 g (1¾ oz)
- [ ] salmon fillet – 125 g (4½ oz)
- [ ] sashimi-grade salmon – 115 g (4 oz)
- [ ] smoked salmon – 340 g (12 oz)
- [ ] prawns (shrimp) – 225 g (8 oz)

DAIRY/EGGS

- [ ] double (heavy) cream
- [ ] almond milk
- [ ] full-fat Greek yoghurt
- [ ] unsalted butter – 190 g (6½ oz)
- [ ] ricotta
- [ ] mozzarella – 115 g (4 oz)
- [ ] burrata
- [ ] parmesan – 135 g (5 oz)
- [ ] gruyere – 160 g (5½ oz)
- [ ] crème fraîche
- [ ] eggs – 12

MISC

- [ ] kelp noodles – 60 g (2 oz)
- [ ] roasted nori strips
- [ ] mixed dried sea vegetables – 15 g (½ oz)
- [ ] sundried tomatoes in oil – 225 g (8 oz)

CHECK TO SEE IF IN PANTRY

- [ ] ghee
- [ ] extra virgin olive oil
- [ ] avocado oil
- [ ] MCT oil
- [ ] coconut oil
- [ ] toasted sesame oil
- [ ] apple cider vinegar
- [ ] chicken stock cube
- [ ] tamari
- [ ] fish sauce
- [ ] almond butter
- [ ] tahini
- [ ] almonds
- [ ] walnuts – 110 g (4 oz)
- [ ] macadamia nuts
- [ ] ground golden linseeds (flax seeds)
- [ ] toasted sesame seeds
- [ ] goji berries – 30 g (1 oz)
- [ ] ground cinnamon
- [ ] cinnamon stick – 1
- [ ] ground cardamom
- [ ] ground nutmeg
- [ ] ground cumin
- [ ] dried oregano
- [ ] ground turmeric
- [ ] dried bay leaf
- [ ] chilli flakes
- [ ] dried chilli de arbol or any dried chilli – 1
- [ ] dried ancho chilli – 1
- [ ] almond flour
- [ ] sukrin gold
- [ ] monkfruit sweetener
- [ ] Dijon mustard

WEEK 4 PREP

Check to see if you have any of these items already made and if not, add ingredients to your shopping list.

BASICS
(these are items that you should have pre-prepped as they will last a while)

- [ ] Pickling Liquid (p. 72)
- [ ] Keto Pancake Base mix (p. 88)
- [ ] Keto 'Oat'meal Base (p. 86)
- [ ] Seeded Keto Bread (p. 84), unless frozen or left over
- [ ] Coconut Flax Granola (p. 172)
- [ ] Harissa (p. 78)

PREP

- [ ] Dry ingredients for Nutty Porridge (p. 160)
- [ ] Grind macadamias for Macadamia Nut 'Oat'meal (p. 158)
- [ ] Cauliflower for Cauli-rice (p. 72)
- [ ] Cauliflower Pizza Crust (p. 92)
- [ ] Zoodles (p. 68)
- [ ] Marinate prawns (shrimp) for Prawns with Lime over Zoodles (p. 158)

MAKE

- [ ] Sundried Tomato Pesto (p. 82)
- [ ] Pozole (156)
- [ ] Tahini Herb Dressing (p. 76)
- [ ] Bacon strips for Frisee & Bacon Salad with Gruyere (p. 160)
- [ ] Golden Milk (p. 90)

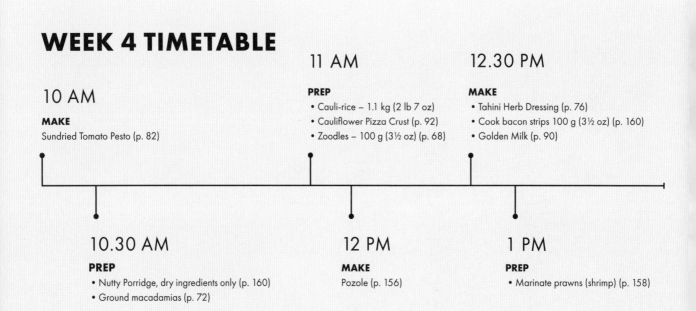

WEEK 4 TIMETABLE

10 AM

MAKE
Sundried Tomato Pesto (p. 82)

10.30 AM

PREP
- Nutty Porridge, dry ingredients only (p. 160)
- Ground macadamias (p. 72)

11 AM

PREP
- Cauli-rice – 1.1 kg (2 lb 7 oz)
- Cauliflower Pizza Crust (p. 92)
- Zoodles – 100 g (3½ oz) (p. 68)

12 PM

MAKE
Pozole (p. 156)

12.30 PM

MAKE
- Tahini Herb Dressing (p. 76)
- Cook bacon strips 100 g (3½ oz) (p. 160)
- Golden Milk (p. 90)

1 PM

PREP
- Marinate prawns (shrimp) (p. 158)

COOK ZOODLES

1. Make zoodles (p. 68), then toss in salt. Leave for 30 minutes

2. Fry in a little oil for 2–3 minutes

3. Or, add zoodles to a lined baking tray and toss in salt

4. Roast in 180°C (350°C) oven for 10–15 minutes

DAY 22

MONDAY

The pickled radishes in today's kale salad lunch can be pre-made ahead at any time, for easy prep.

....

BREAKFAST

Macadamia smoothie bowl with nut butter

SERVINGS: 1
PREP / COOK TIME
15 minutes / 0 minutes

60 ml (¼ cup) almond milk
2 tablespoons full-fat Greek yoghurt
1 tablespoon MCT oil
1 tablespoon almond butter
10 g (⅓ oz) macadamia nuts, toasted
   and chopped

01 Place milk and yoghurt in a blender together with 250 g (9 oz) ice. While the motor is running, slowly add in MCT oil. Pour into a bowl and top with remaining ingredients. Serve.

Nutrition per serving:
349 cals / 33 g fat / 11.9 g carbs /
5.7 g fibre / 6.2 g net carbs / 7.7 g protein

LUNCH

Kale salad with toasted macadamias & tahini herb dressing

SERVINGS: 1
PREP / COOK TIME
15 minutes / 0 minutes

3 radishes, thinly sliced
60 ml (¼ cup) Pickling Liquid (p. 72)
115 g (4 oz) cavolo nero, chopped
1 celery stalk, thinly sliced
4 tablespoons macadamia nuts, toasted
   and chopped
25 g (1 oz) parmesan, shaved
40 ml (1½ fl oz) Tahini Herb Dressing
   (p. 76)
salt and pepper

01 Place radish in a small bowl and pour over pickling liquid. Leave for at least 10 minutes. Arrange cavolo nero and celery in a bowl or container. Top with nuts, parmesan and pickled radish. Drizzle over dressing and season. Serve.

Nutrition per serving:
614 cals / 54 g fat / 19.2 g carbs /
8.5 g fibre / 10.7 g net carbs / 23 g protein

DINNER

Pozole

SERVINGS: 4
PREP / COOK TIME
45 minutes / 3 hours

4 g (⅛ oz) dried chilli de arbol
1 dried ancho chilli
1½ teaspoons salt
450 g (1 lb) boneless pork shoulder
1 tablespoon avocado oil
½ onion, diced
2 teaspoons dried oregano
1 teaspoon ground cumin
1 dried bay leaf
1 chicken stock cube
90 g (1¼ cups) shredded green cabbage
chopped avocado, coriander (cilantro)
   sprigs, sliced radish, to serve

01 Soak chillies in 240 ml (8 fl oz) hot water for 30 minutes. Remove stems and seeds, then puree chilli with soaking water. Salt pork. Heat oil in a Dutch oven, add pork and brown. Add remaining ingredients and enough water to cover pork by 4 cm (1½ in). Cover and simmer for 2½ hours, skimming off fat. Add chilli puree and simmer for 15 minutes. Shred pork using two forks. Serve pozole with toppings. Store any remaining in fridge for another meal.

Nutrition per serving:
409 cals / 30 g fat / 10.2 g carbs /
2.4 g fibre / 7.8 g net carbs / 32 g protein

**MACADAMIA
SMOOTHIE BOWL
WITH NUT BUTTER**

**KALE SALAD WITH TOASTED
MACADAMIAS & TAHINI
HERB DRESSING**

POZOLE

23

TUESDAY

Cooking with a single baking tin, as in today's baked harissa chicken dinner, is not only efficient, but also makes for less washing up.

BREAKFAST

Macadamia nut 'oat'meal

SERVINGS: 1
PREP / COOK TIME
5 minutes / 5 minutes

1 serving Keto 'Oat'meal Base (p. 86)
30 g (1 oz) ground macadamias (p. 72)
½ teaspoon ground cinnamon,
    plus extra to garnish
¼ teaspoon ground nutmeg,
    plus extra to garnish
2 tablespoons double (heavy) cream
1 tablespoon MCT oil
1 teaspoon sukrin gold

01 Place 'oat'meal base in a pan, then add remaining ingredients and heat over medium heat, stirring constantly, for 3–5 minutes. Sprinkle extra cinnamon and nutmeg on top, then serve.

Nutrition per serving:
788 cals / 77 g fat / 20.4 g carbs /
11.2 g fibre / 9.2 g net carbs / 15 g protein

LUNCH

Prawns with lime over zoodles

SERVINGS: 1
PREP / COOK TIME
55 minutes / 5 minutes

½ shallot, very finely chopped
1 garlic clove, very finely chopped
½ teaspoon grated ginger
1 lemongrass stalk, grated
2 teaspoons fish sauce
zest and juice of ½ lime
225 g (8 oz) prawns (shrimp), peeled
    and deveined
salt and pepper
2 tablespoons coconut oil
100 g (3½ oz) Zoodles (p. 68), blanched
1 tablespoon coriander (cilantro) leaves,
    to garnish

01 Combine shallot, garlic, ginger, lemongrass, fish sauce and lime zest and juice in a bowl, then add prawns. Season. Chill for at least 45 minutes, or overnight. Heat oil in a frying pan over medium–high heat. Remove prawns from marinade and add to pan. Cook for 1–2 minutes, until opaque on both sides. Serve with zoodles and garnish with coriander.

Nutrition per serving:
512 cals / 28 g fat / 11.3 g carbs /
2.6 g fibre / 8.7 g net carbs / 56 g protein

DINNER

Baked harissa chicken

SERVINGS: 4
PREP / COOK TIME
55 minutes / 30–45 minutes

1 ½ teaspoons salt
1.5 kg (3 lb 5 oz) whole chicken,
    cut into 8 pieces
4–6 tablespoons Harissa (p. 78)
60 ml (¼ cup) extra virgin olive oil
110 g (4 oz) onion, thinly sliced
1 fennel bulb, thinly sliced
180 g (6½ oz) Brussels sprouts, halved
salt and pepper
lemons wedges, to serve

01 Preheat oven to 220°C (430°F). Salt chicken and set aside for 45 minutes. Combine harissa and 3 tablespoons oil in a large bowl. Add chicken, onion and fennel and toss until coated. In another bowl, toss together Brussels sprouts, remaining oil and salt and pepper. Spread chicken, skin-side up, in a lined baking tin and add the vegetables. Roast for 30–45 minutes, until chicken is cooked through. Serve with lemon wedges. Store any remaining in fridge for another meal.

Nutrition per serving:
445 cals / 28 g fat / 13.2 g carbs /
4.8 g fibre / 8.4 g net carbs / 35.6 g protein

MACADAMIA NUT 'OAT' MEAL

PRAWNS WITH LIME OVER ZOODLES

BAKED HARISSA CHICKEN

DAY

24

WEDNESDAY

A variety of seaweeds – nutrient rich and high in iron – make up the sea vegetables in today's salad lunch.

....

BREAKFAST

Nutty porridge with goji berries

SERVINGS: 1
PREP / COOK TIME
5 minutes / 10 minutes

3 tablespoons almond flour
1 tablespoon ground golden linseeds (flax seeds)
120 ml (4 fl oz) almond milk
1 tablespoon MCT oil
pinch of salt
30 g (1 oz) goji berries

01 Combine flour, linseeds, almond milk, 100 ml (3½ fl oz) water, MCT oil and salt in a pan over medium heat. Stir until mixture begins to thicken. Transfer to a bowl and top with goji berries. Serve immediately.

Nutrition per serving:
307 cals / 28 g fat / 11.8 g carbs /
5.3 g fibre / 6.5 g net carbs / 7.5 g protein

LUNCH

Simple sea vegetable salad with kelp noodles

SERVINGS: 1
PREP / COOK TIME
15 minutes / 0 minutes

4 teaspoons toasted sesame oil
1½ teaspoons tamari
1 teaspoon apple cider vinegar
1 teaspoon sukrin gold
¼ teaspoon grated ginger
60 g (2 oz) kelp noodles
15 g (½ oz) mixed dried sea vegetables, hydrated
20 g (¾ oz) watercress
salt and pepper
toasted sesame seeds, to garnish

01 Mix oil, tamari, vinegar, sukrin gold and ginger together in a large bowl. Add remaining ingredients and toss to combine. Garnish with sesame seeds.

Nutrition per serving:
196 cals / 19 g fat / 12.9 g carbs /
3.6 g fibre / 9.3 g net carbs / 1.9 g protein

DINNER

Frisee & bacon salad with gruyere

SERVINGS: 1
PREP / COOK TIME
15 minutes / 0 minutes

100 g (3½ oz) frisee (curly endive), cut into bite-sized pieces
85 g (3 oz) radicchio, chopped
30 g (1 oz) shaved gruyere
100 g (3½ oz) cooked bacon strips
½ avocado, diced
2 tablespoons lemon juice
3 tablespoons extra virgin olive oil
salt and pepper

01 Arrange frisee and radicchio on a plate or in a bowl. Add remaining ingredients and toss to combine. Season to taste.

Nutrition per serving:
856 cals / 75 g fat / 20.7 g carbs /
8.5 g fibre / 12.2 g net carbs / 31.7 g protein

**NUTTY PORRIDGE
WITH GOJI BERRIES**

**SIMPLE SEA VEGETABLE SALAD
WITH KELP NOODLES**

**FRISEE & BACON SALAD
WITH GRUYERE**

DAY

25

THURSDAY

Just because you are eating keto, doesn't mean you can't have delicious pancakes! Today's breakfast proves it.

BREAKFAST

Lemon ricotta pancakes

SERVINGS: 1
PREP / COOK TIME
5 minutes / 10 minutes

1 serving Keto Pancake Base mix (p. 88)
60 g (¼ cup) ricotta
¼ teaspoon ground cardamom
1 tablespoon lemon zest
2 tablespoons ghee

01 Mix pancake mix and remaining ingredients, except ghee, together in a bowl until well combined. Heat griddle or frying pan and add 1 tablespoon ghee. Pour half the batter into pan and cook until bubbles form on top and bottom browns, about 2–3 minutes. Flip and cook until second side is browned. Remove and repeat with rest of batter and ghee.

Nutrition per serving:
448 cals / 34 g fat / 14 g carbs /
5.9 g fibre / 8.1 g net carbs / 17.5 g protein

LUNCH

Little gem & avocado salad with salmon rillettes

SERVINGS: 1
PREP / COOK TIME
10 minutes / 0 minutes

115 g (4 oz) little gem lettuce leaves
½ avocado, diced
35 g (1¼ oz) thinly sliced red onion
60 g (2 oz) Salmon Rillettes (p. 184)
salt and pepper
2 tablespoons lemon juice
3 tablespoons extra virgin olive oil

01 Arrange little gem lettuce leaves on plate or in a container. Top with avocado, red onion and salmon rillettes. Season, drizzle with lemon juice and olive oil and serve.

Nutrition per serving:
692 cals / 67 g fat / 19 g carbs /
7.2 g fibre / 11.8 g net carbs / 9.3 g protein

DINNER

Kale & Brussels sprouts pizza

SERVINGS: 4–6
PREP / COOK TIME
15 minutes / 15 minutes

30 g (1 oz) kale, finely chopped
115 g (4 oz) Brussels sprouts, thinly shaved
juice of 1 lemon
3 tablespoons extra virgin olive oil
salt and pepper
1 Cauliflower Pizza Crust (p. 92),
   parbaked
115 g (4 oz) mozzarella, grated
190 g (6½ oz) Sundried Tomato Pesto
   (p. 82)
1 teaspoon chilli flakes

01 Preheat oven to 200°C (400°F). Combine kale, Brussels sprouts, lemon juice and 2 tablespoons oil and massage together. Season. Brush remaining oil over crust and top with half the cheese. Distribute kale mixture and dot with pesto. Top with remaining cheese and sprinkle with chilli flakes. Bake for 10–15 minutes, until cheese is bubbly. Serve. Store any remaining in fridge for another meal.

Nutrition per serving:
371 cals / 34 g fat / 8.4 g carbs /
2.2 g fibre / 6.2 g net carbs / 10.8 g protein

LEMON RICOTTA PANCAKES

**LITTLE GEM & AVOCADO SALAD
WITH SALMON RILLETTES**

KALE & BRUSSELS SPROUTS PIZZA

DAY
26

FRIDAY

The golden milk poured over today's granola breakfast can be prepped ahead, simply follow the recipe on page 90.

BREAKFAST

Coconut granola over golden milk

SERVINGS: 1
PREP / COOK TIME
5 minutes / 0 minutes

240 ml (8 fl oz) cold Golden Milk (p. 90)
30 g (1 oz) Coconut Flax Granola (p. 172)

01 Place golden milk in a bowl and serve with granola.

Nutrition per serving:
220 cals / 21 g fat / 10.7 g carbs /
3.6 g fibre / 7.1 g net carbs / 4 g protein

LUNCH

Salmon poke bowls over cauli-rice

SERVINGS: 1
PREP / COOK TIME
15 minutes / 20 minutes

1 teaspoon grated ginger
2 teaspoons toasted sesame oil
1 teaspoon lime juice
1 teaspoon monkfruit sweetener
½ tablespoon tamari
200 g (7 oz) Cauli-rice (p. 72), steamed
115 g (4 oz) sashimi-grade salmon, diced
½ avocado, diced
2 tablespoons crumbled nori strips
1 spring onion (scallion), sliced thinly
   diagonally

01 Combine ginger, oil, lime juice, sweetener and tamari in a small bowl and set aside. Place cauli-rice in a bowl or container and top with salmon and avocado. Drizzle with sauce and garnish with nori and spring onion.

Nutrition per serving:
370 cals / 21 g fat / 21.1 g carbs /
11.6 g fibre / 9.5 g net carbs / 30 g protein

DINNER

'Banh-mi' wraps with beef & herbs

SERVINGS: 1
PREP / COOK TIME
1 hour / 5 minutes

2 tablespoons tamari
1 teaspoon sukrin gold
1 garlic clove, very finely chopped
½ teaspoon toasted sesame oil
100 g (3½ oz) thinly sliced Scotch fillet
   (rib eye) steak
2 spring green leaves (60 g/2 oz),
   rib shaved
50 g (1¾ oz) carrot, julienned
4 thin slices jalapeno chilli
1 spring onion (scallion), sliced into 3 cm
   (1¼ in) pieces
5 g (¼ oz) each coriander (cilantro) leaves
   and Thai basil

01 Mix tamari, sukrin gold, garlic and oil in a bowl. Add beef and chill for 45 minutes. Cook beef in marinade in a pan for 3–4 minutes. To assemble wraps, place leaves on a work surface to make a 30 x 13 cm (12 x 5 in) rectangle. Place beef down middle of wrap, add remaining ingredients and tightly roll up. Slice into 2 pieces.

Nutrition per serving:
271 cals / 13 g fat / 12.2 g carbs /
4.1 g fibre / 8.1 g net carbs / 29 g protein

COCONUT GRANOLA OVER GOLDEN MILK

'BANH-MI' WRAPS
WITH BEEF & HERBS

SALMON POKE BOWLS
OVER CAULI-RICE

SATURDAY

The beef from today's lunch and the sundried tomato pesto from today's dinner, can both be prepped ahead, to reduce your time in the kitchen.

....

BREAKFAST

Crustless ricotta quiche with gruyere & spinach

SERVINGS: 6
PREP / COOK TIME
10 minutes / 20 minutes

2 tablespoons extra virgin olive oil
½ onion (55 g/2 oz), diced
115 g (4 oz) English spinach
8 large eggs, whisked
240 g (8½ oz) ricotta
55 g (2 oz) gruyere, grated
salt and pepper

01 Preheat oven to 180°C (350°C). Heat oil in a large non-stick, ovenproof frying pan. Add onion and cook until translucent. Add spinach and cook for 3–5 minutes, until wilted. Combine egg, cheeses, salt and pepper and pour into pan. Cover for 2–3 minutes. Uncover and bake for 10 minutes or until cooked through. Slice into 6 pieces and serve. Store any remaining slices in fridge for another meal.

Nutrition per serving:
194 cals / 15 g fat / 2.7 g carbs /
0.4 g fibre / 2.3 g net carbs / 12 g protein

LUNCH

Spicy Thai beef salad

SERVINGS: 1
PREP / COOK TIME
1 ¼ hours / 5 minutes

2 tablespoons lime juice
2 tablespoons fish sauce
1 tablespoon grated lemongrass
½ red chilli (or jalapeno), sliced
1 tablespoon sukrin gold
1 tablespoon avocado oil
80 g (2¾ oz) thinly sliced Scotch fillet (rib eye) steak
85 g (3 oz) butter (bibb) lettuce
1 short cucumber, sliced
75 g (2¾ oz) green bell pepper (capsicum), sliced
2 tablespoons each of basil, coriander (cilantro) and mint leaves
1 spring onion (scallion), thinly sliced

01 Combine lime juice, fish sauce, lemongrass, chilli and sukrin gold in a bowl and set aside. Heat oil in a pan over medium–high heat and cook beef for 3–5 minutes, until cooked. Place beef in sauce and chill for 1 hour. (This can be done the night before.) Arrange lettuce on a plate or in a container, add cucumber and bell pepper. Add beef and sauce and top with remaining ingredients.

Nutrition per serving:
252 cals / 12 g fat / 16 g carbs /
3.4 g fibre / 12.6 g net carbs / 24.7 g protein

DINNER

Almond-crusted fish with Brussels sprouts

SERVINGS: 1
PREP / COOK TIME
15 minutes / 20 minutes

30 g (1 oz) almond flour
1 egg, whisked
3 tablespoons almonds, toasted and finely chopped
salt and pepper
125 g (4½ oz) salmon fillet
5 tablespoons avocado oil
65 g (2¼ oz) Brussels sprouts, halved or quartered
50 g (1¾ oz) Sundried Tomato Pesto (p. 82)

01 Place flour, egg and almonds in separate bowls. Season salmon, then dip in flour, then egg, then almonds. Heat 2 tablespoons oil in a large frying pan and cook Brussels sprouts, stirring occasionally, until cooked. Season and remove from pan. Add remaining oil and pan-fry salmon for 5–8 minutes on each side. Plate Brussels sprouts and salmon and top with pesto.

Nutrition per serving:
951 cals / 84 g fat / 16.1 g carbs /
6.7 g fibre / 9.4 g net carbs / 38.7 g protein

**CRUSTLESS RICOTTA QUICHE
WITH GRUYERE & SPINACH**

SPICY THAI BEEF SALAD

**ALMOND-CRUSTED FISH
WITH BRUSSELS SPROUTS**

SUNDAY

Roasted tomatoes, like those used in today's steak dinner, are a great way to include more umami flavour in the keto diet.

BREAKFAST

Ham & cheese omelette

SERVINGS: 1
PREP / COOK TIME
10 minutes / 5 minutes

salt and pepper
3 large eggs, whisked
2 tablespoons butter
75 g (2¾ oz) gruyere, grated
50 g (1¾ oz) ham, diced
1 tablespoon finely chopped chives

01 Season egg. Heat butter in a large non-stick frying pan over medium heat and add egg. Tilt pan to spread egg mixture out evenly. When egg begins to firm up, about 2–3 minutes, add cheese and ham. Fold egg in half and transfer to a plate. Season and top with chives.

Nutrition per serving:
797 cals / 65 g fat / 3.1 g carbs /
0.1 g fibre / 3 g net carbs / 50 g protein

LUNCH

Salmon rillettes & crudité platter

SERVINGS: 1
PREP / COOK TIME
10 minutes / 0 minutes

60 g (2 oz) Salmon Rillettes (p. 184)
1 slice Seeded Keto Bread (p. 84)
100 g (3½ oz) radishes, quartered
2 celery stalks, sliced into spears
1 head of witlof (Belgian endive/chicory), leaves separated

01 Arrange all ingredients on a plate and serve.

Nutrition per serving:
446 cals / 37 g fat / 18 g carbs /
11 g fibre / 7 g net carbs / 15 g protein

DINNER

Harissa hanger steak

SERVINGS: 1
PREP / COOK TIME
35 minutes / 20 minutes

15 g (½ oz) Harissa (p. 78)
85 g (3 oz) hanger (skirt) steak
80 g (2¾ oz) cherry tomatoes
60 ml (¼ cup) extra virgin olive oil
salt and pepper
1 teaspoon chopped thyme, plus extra to garnish
55 g (2 oz) burrata

01 Preheat oven to 190°C (375°F). Spread harissa over steak and marinate at room temperature for 30 minutes. Meanwhile, toss cherry tomatoes with oil, salt and pepper and thyme. Place on a lined baking tray and bake for 10–15 minutes, until tomatoes start to burst. Cook steak in a chargrill pan to your liking. Serve with cherry tomatoes and burrata, and garnished with thyme. Season.

Nutrition per serving:
945 cals / 86 g fat / 8.5 g carbs /
2.8 g fibre / 5.7 g net carbs / 35 g protein

HAM & CHEESE
OMELETTE

SALMON RILLETTES
& CRUDITÉ PLATTER

HARISSA HANGER
STEAK

DRINKS & SNACKS: INTRODUCTION

If you eat three meals a day according to the 28-day meal plan, there is probably not a lot of flexibility in terms of consuming additional items if you want to get into and stay in ketosis. But there are lots of reasons why you might want to make and eat the recipes in this chapter – from meal swaps to dessert replacements to additional sustenance on workout days – which includes snacks, smoothies, sweets, savoury bites, fat bombs and dips and spreads.

SNACKS ON HAND

Having pre-made snacks on hand is an easy, keto-friendly way to quickly curb hunger without turning to processed, carb-heavy, sugar-filled convenience foods, especially when you are on the go.

Trail mix

MAKES: 400 G (14 OZ)
SERVINGS: 12
PREP / COOK TIME
10 minutes / 45–60 minutes

110 g (4 oz) pecans, roughly chopped
130 g (4½ oz) brazil nuts, roughly chopped
70 g (2½ oz) almonds, roughly chopped
1 tablespoon linseeds (flax seeds)
1 egg white
½ teaspoon salt
2 teaspoons monkfruit sweetener
2 tablespoons coconut oil

01 Preheat oven to 160°C (320°F). Toss all ingredients together in a large bowl. On a lined baking tray, spread mix in an even layer. Bake for 45–60 minutes, rotating baking tray halfway through. Remove and cool before serving. Store in an airtight container for up to a month.

Nutrition per serving:
196 cals / 20 g fat / 4.9 g carbs / 2.8 g fibre / 2.1 g net carbs / 4.1 g protein

Coconut flax granola

MAKES: 675 G (1½ LB)
SERVINGS: 24
PREP / COOK TIME
10 minutes / 45 minutes

135 g (5 oz) macadamia nuts, chopped
135 g (5 oz) hazelnuts, chopped
110 g (4 oz) pecans, chopped
40 g (1½ oz) pumpkin seeds, chopped
50 g (1¾ oz) ground golden linseeds (flax seeds)
40 g (⅔ cup) shredded coconut
70 g (2½ oz) erythritol
1 egg white
60 g (2 oz) butter, melted
salt

01 Preheat oven to 150°C (300°F). Combine all ingredients in a large bowl and stir. Spread in an even layer on a baking tray. Bake for 45 minutes, stirring every 15 minutes. Cool. Add salt to taste. Store in an airtight container for up to a month.

Nutrition per serving:
155 cals / 15 g fat / 6.8 g carbs / 2.5 g fibre/ 4.3 g net carbs / 3 g protein

Nori mixed nuts

MAKES: 400 G (14 OZ)
SERVINGS: 15
PREP / COOK TIME
5 minutes / 30 minutes

135 g (5 oz) macadamia nuts
130 g (4½ oz) almonds, chopped
65 g (2¼ oz) cashews
5 g (¼ oz) nori strips
1 tablespoon toasted sesame seeds
2 teaspoons gochugaru or aleppo pepper
2 teaspoons sukrin gold
60 ml (¼ cup) olive oil
½ teaspoon salt

01 Preheat oven to 150°C (300°F). Combine all ingredients in a bowl and toss to coat. Spread mixture in an even layer on a lined baking tray. Bake for 30 minutes, stirring halfway through. Cool. Add more salt to taste. Store in an airtight container for up to a month.

Nutrition per serving:
38 cals / 3.2 g fat / 7.4 g carbs / 4.3 g fibre / 3.1 g net carbs / 3.6 g protein

COCONUT FLAX GRANOLA

NORI MIXED NUTS

TRAIL MIX

SWEETS

Sugar is off limits in the keto diet, but that doesn't mean you can't have anything dessert-like. Dark chocolate, shredded coconut and mixed berries can help satisfy a sweet tooth within the keto parameters.

Mixed berry coconut ice bars

MAKES: 10
PREP / FREEZE TIME
10 minutes / 3–4 hours

200 ml (7 fl oz) coconut milk
200 ml (7 fl oz) almond milk
30 g (1 oz) raspberries
35 g (1¼ oz) blackberries
60 g (2 oz) monkfruit
   sweetener

01 Combine all ingredients in a blender and blend until smooth. Pour into popsicle moulds, leaving 3 cm (1¼ in) headspace. Freeze and serve when fully frozen.

Nutrition per serving:
38 cals / 3.2 g fat / 7.4 g carbs / 1.6 g fibre / 5.8 g net carbs / 5 g protein

Coconut chocolate bon bons with nuts

MAKES: 4
PREP / COOK TIME
15 minutes / 0 minutes

8 g (⅓ oz) shredded coconut
2 tablespoons macadamia nuts,
   toasted and finely chopped
1 tablespoon coconut butter,
   melted
1 tablespoon dark
   (unsweetened) cocoa powder

01 Place all ingredients in a food processor and pulse until just combined. Roll into 4 cm (1½ in) balls and refrigerate until firm. Serve. Store in fridge for up to a month.

Nutrition per serving:
242 cals / 23 g fat / 9 g carbs / 6.3 g fibre / 2.7 g net carbs / 3.3 g protein

Macadamia nut bark

MAKES: 12 PIECES
PREP / COOK TIME
15 minutes / 0 minutes

225 g (8 oz) dark chocolate
   (at least 70% cocoa solids),
   roughly chopped
130 g (4½ oz) macadamia
   nuts, toasted and chopped
1 teaspoon coarse sea salt

01 Place chocolate in a heatproof bowl set over a pan of simmering water. Stir frequently until chocolate has almost melted. Remove from heat and keep stirring until melted. Pour chocolate onto a lined baking tray and spread into an even layer. Quickly scatter with nuts and coarse salt and cool for 1 hour until chocolate sets. Break into bark pieces and store in zip-lock bag at room temperature for up to 3 days.

Nutrition per serving:
192 cals / 16 g fat / 10.1 g carbs / 2.9 g fibre / 7.2 g net carbs / 2.3 g protein

MACADAMIA NUT BARK

MIXED BERRY COCONUT ICE BARS

**COCONUT CHOCOLATE
BON BONS WITH NUTS**

SAVOURY BITES

The longer you eat keto, the less you will crave sweets. These savoury snacks are good for the days when you have a bit more time to prep.

Devilled eggs

SERVINGS: 4
PREP / COOK TIME
15 minutes / 0 minutes

4 hard-boiled eggs (p. 178), halved
1 teaspoon Dijon mustard
2 tablespoons Avocado Oil Mayo (p. 74)
½ teaspoon smoked paprika
1 teaspoon finely chopped chives, plus extra to garnish
salt and pepper

01 Carefully remove cooked yolks into a bowl, setting aside the egg whites. Mash yolks and add remaining ingredients. Season with salt and pepper. Pipe or spoon yolk mixture back into egg whites and serve immediately. Or, store in fridge for up to 2 days.

Nutrition per serving:
139 cals / 12 g fat / 0.7 g carbs / 0.1 g fibre / 0.6 g net carbs / 6.4 g protein

Steamed artichokes with garlic aioli

SERVINGS: 4
PREP / COOK TIME
10 minutes / 45 minutes

2 artichokes (250 g/9 oz), prepared and steamed (p. 137)
95 ml (3¼ fl oz) Garlic Aioli (p. 82)

01 Gently pull away artichoke petals and enjoy with aioli.

Nutrition per serving:
204 cals / 19 g fat / 7.8 g carbs / 6.5 g fibre / 1.3 g net carbs / 2.7 g protein

Haloumi sticks with herb pesto

SERVINGS: 6
PREP / COOK TIME
5 minutes / 15 minutes

1 tablespoon extra virgin olive oil
250 g (9 oz) haloumi, sliced
225 g (8 oz) Herb Pesto (p. 82)

01 Heat oil in a frying pan over medium heat and fry haloumi for 15 minutes, or until browned on both sides. Serve with herb pesto.

Nutrition per serving:
464 cals / 42 g fat / 2.3 g carbs / 0.5 g fibre / 1.8 g net carbs / 9 g protein

DEVILLED EGGS

HALOUMI STICKS WITH HERB PESTO

STEAMED ARTICHOKES
WITH GARLIC AIOLI

BOILED EGG HOW-TO

....

To cook perfect eggs, remove your eggs from the fridge before cooking, then bring a medium saucepan of water to the boil. Carefully, lower the egg(s) into the boiling water and cook to your liking.

BOIL FOR 5–6 MINUTES FOR SOFT-BOILED
BOIL FOR 7–8 MINUTES FOR A JAMMY EGG
BOIL FOR 10–12 MINUTES FOR HARD-BOILED

If consuming straight away, peel the just-boiled egg/s under cold running water, so not to burn your fingers.

You can store your cooked egg/s in their shells for up to a week in the fridge. Just remember to keep them separate from raw eggs, so you don't have a mix-up.

The average person can eat up to 10 eggs per day on the keto diet, as they are high in protein and contain zero net carbs.

Nutrition per egg:
78 cals / 5 g fat / 0 g carbs / 0 g fibre / 0 g net carbs / 6 g protein

SOFT-BOILED

JAMMY EGG

HARD-BOILED

FAT BOMBS

As getting enough fat is the most crucial element of eating keto, fat bombs are an important part of your snack arsenal. Not to mention how tasty they are!

Lemon, cardamom & coconut butter balls

MAKES: 10
PREP / COOK TIME
20 minutes / 0 minutes

80 ml (⅓ cup) crème fraîche
120 g (4½ oz) coconut butter
2 tablespoons coconut oil
2 teaspoons lemon juice
grated zest from ½ lemon
1 teaspoon monkfruit
   sweetener
½ teaspoon ground cardamom
40 g (⅔ cup) shredded
   coconut

01 Place crème fraîche, butter and oil in a large bowl and mix until combined. Add remaining ingredients, except coconut, and roll into 10 balls. Roll balls in coconut to coat. Store in an airtight container in fridge for up to 2 days.

Nutrition per serving:
274 cals / 27 g fat / 8 g carbs /
4.6 g fibre / 3.4 g net carbs /
2.3 g protein

Pumpkin fat bombs

MAKES: 10
PREP / CHILL TIME
20 minutes / 2 hours

60 g (2 oz) coconut butter
115 g (4 oz) cream cheese
60 g (2 oz) tinned pumpkin
   puree
120 g (4½ oz) ground pecans
   (p. 72)
1 teaspoon vanilla extract
120 ml (4 fl oz) whipping
   cream
3 tablespoons sukrin gold
1½ teaspoons ground
   cinnamon
½ teaspoon ground ginger
½ teaspoon ground cloves
½ teaspoon ground nutmeg

01 Place butter, cream cheese and pumpkin puree in a large bowl and mix until combined. Add remaining ingredients. Roll into 10 balls or spoon into moulds and chill for 2 hours until hardened. Store in an airtight container in fridge for up to 2 days.

Nutrition per serving:
221 cals / 22 g fat / 7.4 g carbs /
2.1 g fibre / 5.3 g net carbs /
3 g protein

Dark chocolate fat bombs

MAKES: 10
PREP / CHILL TIME
20 minutes / 2 hours

130 g (4½ oz) ground
   macadamias (p. 72)
3 tablespoons coconut oil
1 tablespoon MCT oil
½ teaspoon vanilla extract
50 g (1¾ oz) monkfruit
   sweetener
2 tablespoons dark cacao
   powder

01 Place ground nuts, coconut oil and MCT oil in a large bowl and mix until combined. Add remaining ingredients. Roll mixture into 10 balls and chill for 2 hours until hardened. Store in an airtight container in fridge for up to 2 days.

Nutrition per serving:
148 cals / 16 g fat / 7.2 g carbs /
1.4 g fibre / 5.8 g net carbs /
1 g protein

LEMON CARDAMOM &
COCONUT BUTTER BALLS

DARK CHOCOLATE FAT BOMBS

PUMPKIN
FAT BOMBS

DIPS & SPREADS

These dips and spreads make great snacks and are used in a number of daily recipes. They are also wonderful dishes to bring to picnics or dinner parties to ensure you have something keto-friendly to eat.

Beetroot dip

MAKES: 240 ML (8 FL OZ) / SERVINGS: 10
PREP / COOK TIME
15 minutes / 0 minutes

3 large beetroot (beets)
   (250 g/9 oz), roasted
   and peeled
30 g (1 oz) walnuts, chopped
1 teaspoon ground cumin
2 garlic cloves, crushed
120 ml (4 fl oz) tahini
2 teaspoons lemon juice
70 ml (2¼ fl oz) extra virgin
   olive oil
salt and pepper

01 Place all ingredients, except olive oil, in a food processor or blender and blend until smooth. Add olive oil in a steady stream until creamy. Season with salt and pepper. Store in a container in fridge for 4–5 days.

Nutrition per serving:
166 cals / 16 g fat / 5.7 g carbs / 2 g fibre / 3.7 g net carbs / 3 g protein

Labneh with dukkah

MAKES: 175 G (6 OZ)
SERVINGS: 6–8
PREP / COOK TIME
15 minutes / 0 minutes

60 g (2 oz) hazelnuts, toasted
60 g (2 oz) pistachios, toasted
30 g (1 oz) walnuts, toasted
2 tablespoons toasted
   sesame seeds
1 tablespoon coriander seeds,
   toasted
1 teaspoon cumin seeds, toasted
1 teaspoon fennel seeds, toasted
pinch of dried mint
120 g (4½ oz) labneh

01 Combine dry ingredients in a food processor and pulse until coarsely ground. Sprinkle some dukkah over the labneh and store the leftovers in a jar in the pantry.

Nutrition per serving:
395 cals / 36 g fat / 11.6 g carbs / 5 g fibre / 6.6 g net carbs / 10.7 g protein

Chicken liver mousse

SERVINGS: 12
PREP / COOK TIME
20 minutes / 20 minutes

4 tablespoons unsalted butter
2 tablespoons bacon fat
½ large onion, thinly sliced
salt and pepper
450 g (1 lb) chicken livers,
   cleaned
2 thyme sprigs
½ dried bay leaf
3 tablespoons red wine
¼ teaspoon ground cinnamon
¼ teaspoon star anise
160 ml (5½ fl oz) double (heavy)
   cream
115 g (4 oz) cream cheese, cubed

01 Heat butter and fat in a pan and caramelise onion. Season. Set aside. Wipe out pan and fry livers until browned on each side. Add herbs and wine and cook until liquid has evaporated. Discard herbs, then blitz livers in blender with remaining ingredients until smooth. Season. Press into mould or jar. Chill in fridge for up to a week.

Nutrition per serving:
210 cals / 17 g fat / 3.2 g carbs / 0.5 g fibre/ 2.7 g net carbs / 10.6 g protein

CHICKEN LIVER MOUSSE

LABNEH WITH DUKKAH

BEETROOT DIP

MORE DIPS & SPREADS

Guacamole

MAKES: 365 G (13 OZ)
SERVINGS: 4
PREP / COOK TIME
10 minutes / 0 minutes

2 avocados
2 garlic cloves, very finely
   chopped
1 tablespoon very finely
   chopped jalapeno
1 teaspoon ground cumin
60 ml (¼ cup) lime juice
1 tablespoon MCT oil
3 tablespoons finely chopped
   coriander (cilantro) leaves
salt and pepper

01 Mash avocado, garlic, jalapeno
and cumin together in a bowl. Add
lime juice and MCT oil and mix
through. Fold in coriander. Season
to taste.

Nutrition per serving:
151 cals / 14 g fat / 8 g carbs /
4.9 g fibre / 3.1 g net carbs /
2 g protein

Salmon rillettes

MAKES: 725 G (1 LB 10 OZ)
SERVINGS: 12
PREP / COOK TIME
15 minutes / 0 minutes

170 g (6 oz) unsalted butter
90 g (3 oz) shallot, finely diced
115 g (4 oz) crème fraîche
340 g (12 oz) smoked salmon,
   roughly chopped
grated zest of 1 lemon
12 g (½ oz) chives, finely
   chopped
salt and pepper

01 Place butter, shallot and crème
fraîche in a food processor and
pulse until combined. Add remaining
ingredients and pulse until chopped
and chunky. Season.

Nutrition per serving:
173 cals / 16 g fat / 1.6 g carbs /
0.3 g fibre / 1.3 g net carbs /
5.8 g protein

Herbed cheese spread

MAKES: 260 G (9 OZ)
SERVINGS: 6–8
PREP / COOK TIME
10 minutes / 0 minutes

110 g (4 oz) cream cheese,
   at room temperature
110 g (4 oz) goat's cheese,
   at room temperature
1 tablespoon extra virgin olive
   oil
2 roasted garlic cloves (p. 72),
   smashed
3 tablespoons chopped parsley
1 tablespoon chopped dill
1 tablespoon chopped chives
salt and pepper

01 Place ingredients in a food
processor and pulse until well
combined. Season to taste.

Nutrition per serving:
119 cals / 11 g fat / 1.3 g carbs /
0.1 g fibre / 1.2 g net carbs /
4.1 g protein

HERBED CHEESE SPREAD

SALMON RILLETTES

GUACAMOLE

SMOOTHIES & DRINKS

These smoothies and drinks can be a quick and easy breakfast alternative, when you want to shake things up.

Avocado nut smoothie

SERVINGS: 1
PREP / COOK TIME
5 minutes / 0 minutes

¼ avocado
3 tablespoons almond butter
240 ml (8 fl oz) almond milk
1 teaspoon chia seeds
1 tablespoon MCT oil

01 Place ingredients in a blender and blend until smooth. Serve immediately.

Nutrition per serving:
513 cals / 49 g fat / 14.6 g carbs / 8.3 g fibre / 6.3 g net carbs / 12.5 g protein

Raspberry chocolate smoothie

SERVINGS: 1
PREP / COOK TIME
5 minutes / 0 minutes

60 g (2 oz) frozen raspberries
1 tablespoon cacao powder
1 tablespoon MCT oil
3 tablespoons full-fat Greek yoghurt
180 ml (6 fl oz) almond milk
2 tablespoons ground linseeds (flax seeds)

01 Place ingredients in a blender and blend until smooth. Serve immediately.

Nutrition per serving:
300 cals / 23 g fat / 18.4 g carbs / 9.1 g fibre / 9.3 g net carbs / 10 g protein

Mint chocolate chip smoothie

SERVINGS: 1
PREP / COOK TIME
5 minutes / 0 minutes

½ avocado
30 g (1 oz) baby spinach
10 g (⅓ oz) mint
1 teaspoon monkfruit sweetener
1 scoop protein powder
120 ml (4 fl oz) almond milk
110 g (4 oz) ice cubes
1 teaspoon cacao nibs

01 Place all ingredients, except cacao nibs, in a blender and blend until smooth. Add cacao nibs and stir to combine. Serve immediately.

Nutrition per serving:
213 cals / 17 g fat / 14.6 g carbs / 6.8 g fibre / 7.8 g net carbs / 8.3 g protein

AVOCADO NUT
SMOOTHIE

MINT CHOCOLATE CHIP
SMOOTHIE

RASPBERRY
CHOCOLATE SMOOTHIE

MORE SMOOTHIES & DRINKS

Coffee cacao smoothie

SERVINGS: 1
PREP / COOK TIME
5 minutes / 0 minutes

120 ml (4 fl oz) coffee, at room temperature
120 ml (4 fl oz) coconut milk
1 tablespoon cacao powder
1 tablespoon coconut oil
110 g (4 oz) ice cubes

01 Place ingredients in a blender and blend until smooth. Serve immediately.

Nutrition per serving:
336 cals / 32 g fat / 6.8 g carbs / 1.6 g fibre / 5.2 g net carbs / 2.8 g protein

Matcha latte with coconut milk

SERVINGS: 1
PREP / COOK TIME
5 minutes / 0 minutes

120 ml (4 fl oz) almond milk, hot
120 ml (4 fl oz) coconut milk, hot
2 teaspoons matcha (green tea) powder
1 tablespoon MCT oil or coconut oil

01 Place ingredients in a blender and blend until frothy. Serve immediately. Alternatively, stir in a cup and serve.

Nutrition per serving:
333 cals / 33 g fat / 4.4 g carbs / 0.5 g fibre / 3.9 g net carbs / 2 g protein

Spicy chai

SERVINGS: 1
PREP / COOK TIME
5 minutes / 15 minutes

240 ml (8 fl oz) almond milk
2–3 saffron threads
1 tablespoon finely chopped ginger
¼ teaspoon cloves
½ teaspoon cardamom pods
1 cinnamon stick
½ teaspoon black peppercorns
sukrin gold, to sweeten (optional)

01 Combine all ingredients, except sukrin, in a small pan and bring to a low simmer for 10–15 minutes, stirring occasionally. Sweeten, if liked. Pour into a cup and serve.

Nutrition per serving:
47 cals / 3 g fat / 3.8 g carbs / 0.4 g fibre / 3.4 g net carbs / 1.7 g protein

COFFEE CACAO SMOOTHIE

MATCHA LATTE WITH
COCONUT MILK

SPICY CHAI

INDEX

ACKNOWLEDGEMENTS

Lisa Butterworth: I've always loved food, but I didn't truly learn how to cook, savour and appreciate it until I met Caroline Hwang. From the potluck Friendsgivings she orchestrated in the tiny Brooklyn apartment we shared, to the al fresco dinners she serves up now that we both live in LA, Caroline's meals, and the people I get to share them with, have taught me what life is truly about – thank you Caroline! Thanks to Catie Ziller for making this fun project possible, to Kathy Steer for her editing and to Michelle Tilly for working her design magic on all of it. Thanks to Juliz Stotz, and the rest of the photo and styling team, for making these pages look good enough to eat. And extra special thanks to Ines Kivimaki, for showing us the keto ropes when we were first getting started. I'm forever grateful to my toddler-watching parents, Pete and Jan Butterworth, and future in-laws, Yolanda and Romualdo Avila; to my toddler himself, for reminding me that time is precious and good health gives us more of it; and to my partner Manuel, for being willing – and happy – to eat just about anything.

Caroline Hwang: Thank you to Catie Ziller for giving us this book. Thanks to my writing partner, Lisa Butterworth, for making my life easier. Thanks to Kathy Steer for always making sure my recipes and words make sense! Thanks to Michelle for always creating a beautiful book. And my appreciation is endless to Amy Lipnis for making the food pop with her props and surfaces and talent. Same goes for my partner in crime, Julia Stotz, for keeping me organised and making the food look good. I couldn't have done this without the help I received from Jessica Darakjian and Naomi Beauxprey.

First published in French in 2020 by Hachette Livre (Marabout)
58, rue Jean Bleuzen, 92178, Vanves, France

Copyright © Hachette Livre (Marabout) 2020
The rights of the authors have been asserted.

This edition published in 2024 by Smith Street Books
Naarm (Melbourne) | Australia | smithstreetbooks.com

ISBN: 978-1-9230-4957-4

Publisher: Paul McNally
Managing editor: Lucy Heaver
Editor: Ariana Klepac
Photographer: Julia Stotz
Food stylist: Amy Lipnis
Designer: Michelle Tilly
Proofreader: Pam Dunne

Printed & bound in China by C&C Offset Printing Co., Ltd.

Book 352
10 9 8 7 6 5 4 3 2 1